GOD's AIR FORCE

GOD's AIR FORCE

My Tour of Duty With
ADVENTIST WORLD RADIO

ALLEN STEELE

Pacific Press®
Publishing Association
Nampa, Idaho | www.pacificpress.com

Cover design: Trent Truman
Cover illustrations: GettyImages.com
Interior design: Aaron Troia

Copyright© 2023 by Pacific Press® Publishing Association
Printed in the United States of America
All rights reserved

The author assumes full responsibility for the accuracy of all facts and quotations as cited in this book.

Unless otherwise noted, all Scripture quotations are from the King James Version of the Bible.

To order additional copies of this book, call toll-free 1-800-765-6955, or visit AdventistBookCenter.com.

ISBN 978-0-8163-6910-2

January 2023

Contents

Foreword	7
Acknowledgments	9
A Note From the Author	11
Introduction	13
1. Learning to Live	19
2. Finding Myself	26
3. Three Loves	33
4. On the Air	40
5. The World Responds	47
6. Secret Christians	52
7. Life in Portugal	58
8. Can You Stay Another Year?	65
9. Challenging the Giant	71
10. Fall of the Dictator	78
11. Trials and Triumphs	83

12. A Stint in Local Radio	88
13. Asia Calling	95
14. Pulling It All Together	103
15. The Trumpet Sounds	110
16. Island Life and Beyond	116
17. Touching Hearts in China	125
18. Storms out of the Blue	133
19. Island Farewell	138
20. Europe Landing	143
21. The Banner Years	150
22. A British Sojourn	159
23. At Home in England	165
24. A South Pacific Assignment	170
25. Time in Oz	176
26. Back in the USA	180
27. The Navajo Call	188
How You Can Support Adventist World Radio	192

Foreword

In this book, God's power is on full display as you see how He has blessed Adventist World Radio (AWR). This story of the development of an innovative idea to blanket the world with God's biblical truth through radio broadcasts will thrill your heart. In *God's Air Force*, Allen Steele provides a personal and professional view of the development of AWR from its inception more than fifty years ago to its current mighty evangelistic outreach, which uses many different media formats, including shortwave and middle wave broadcasts, the internet, YouTube, "Godpods," cell phone evangelism, public evangelism, and more. This exciting book takes you behind the scenes to the time when AWR was just beginning. The establishment of a radio production office in Portugal was the start of something extraordinary, which God has blessed enormously.

The AWR story is also intertwined with the lives of Allen and Andrea Steele, who have served magnificently through God's power. Allen adds many personal stories and anecdotes, making you feel part of the story as it develops. The personal interest aspects of how God opened doors for the broadcasting of the Advent message in these last days of Earth's history will encourage you to have an evangelistic heart and help you to consider what you can do for the Lord in Total Member Involvement. You may even be motivated to contribute to AWR and its amazing outreach around the globe.

We give glory to God for the progress that AWR has made in proclaiming the three angels' messages worldwide in so many languages. He uses people to accomplish His plans! As you read this book, you will be captivated by seeing how the Lord has directed AWR's work. You will also discover that you can be part of AWR's outreach initiative: AWR360 Broadcast to Baptism.

AWR has developed a keen focus on fulfilling the Great Commission of Matthew 28: to go into all the world. It does this with the enormous cooperation of many studios, producing programs in multiple languages, reaching people in the hardest-to-reach places, and using the languages that are most familiar to listeners.

I have a long history with AWR and heartily support it. My father was instrumental in helping AWR get started many years ago, and it has been my privilege to be an AWR board member for twenty-two years, serving for ten of those years as board chair. I have personally seen how God has used AWR in a mighty manner to reach thousands of people through the airwaves and in many formats, combined with public evangelism, to bring people to the foot of the cross and Christ's Advent message during the final countdown of Earth's history.

I have known Allen and Andrea Steele for many years and think very highly of them both. They are some of God's greatest "Air Force" evangelistic pioneers, and they have been a tremendous blessing to the Seventh-day Adventist Church as we share with the world the wonderful news of Christ's soon return. You will be blessed by reading this fascinating story of God's leading in the work of AWR, which is a vital part of Total Member Involvement in "Reaching the World" through the power of the Holy Spirit.

Let us all respond to God's call by saying, "Yes, Lord, I will go and, in anticipation of the second coming of our Lord and Savior, will share the three angels' messages with the people of this globe in every way possible—including AWR." Enjoy this engaging account of God's direct leading of Adventist World Radio and His people in these last days of Earth's history!

Ted N. C. Wilson, President
General Conference of Seventh-day Adventists

Acknowledgments

My gratitude goes out to a number of people who have greatly encouraged me in preparing this book. First, I thank my wife, Andrea, who has permitted me to include her thoughts and words throughout the Adventist World Radio (AWR) story. Since the book is written in story form, her comments add to the interest of how we worked together in making decisions, and her thoughts express our joys and stresses during our term of duty with AWR.

Second, my thanks to General Conference President Ted Wilson, who, after his father, took on the mantle as our chief encourager while we served the church. Whenever he and his wife, Nancy, happened to be at the same place as we were, they would take time from their busy schedule to look us up.

Third, our appreciation goes to the AWR leadership team. President Duane McKey is always encouraging and urging us on to bigger and greater things. It is the hallmark of his leadership style. Sue Hinkle, AWR's outreach manager, has always been there to encourage and support. Vice President Ray Allen always makes time to provide soft-spoken, pastoral backing. The AWR Ambassador team also constantly expresses their support.

One person at AWR merits special thanks: Daniela Goia, senior office assistant. She was assigned as my helper in searching the archives for information and photos for this book, making it much more than just a history book.

Finally, my thanks go to all my AWR colleagues through the years. I was constantly impressed with their professionalism and dedication to ministry. My association with each of them made life exciting and meaningful as we walked together in the path of service, witnessing the Lord's miracles. I could start listing their names, but it would require another book. I hope this book—my story and theirs—meets the level of excellence they deserve.

A Note From the Author

Longtime friends of Adventist World Radio (AWR) will be aware that many of the chapters in this book include accounts from my earlier book *Loud Let It Ring!*, written in celebration of the twenty-fifth anniversary of the first broadcasts. Because of my desire to present the AWR story in its entirety, and for readers who have not read the earlier book, I felt it best to repeat those chapters so that the first fifty years are consolidated in one place.

I also would point out that a section of the AWR story is missing in this book. During my eight years while working in the South Pacific, I was not well informed of the organization's activities. Since I wrote this book from the perspective based on my personal involvement with AWR, I felt I could not include information that I did not experience. I hope someone involved during those years will write that history one day.

The AWR story is important for the Seventh-day Adventist Church. It inspires admiration for God, who leads His people to imagine and plan big to accomplish the task that He assigned. It is my sincere hope that it will also inspire the church's younger generations to search for their place in His plan.

Introduction

Adventist World Radio (AWR) began broadcasts from Sines, Portugal, on October 1, 1971, and during the succeeding years, it would become one of the largest and most widely known international Christian broadcast organizations in the world. I was there on that day.

I will tell you the story of AWR as I lived it, from the time that the first broadcasts went on air through AWR's first fifty years of history. The church is God's army, but I call AWR "God's air force."

The story of AWR would not be complete if I did not share some of the history leading up to that exciting day when I had the privilege of putting the first programs on the air over Europe, the Middle East, and North Africa. As you read of the events leading to that historic date in 1971, you will see how God worked miraculously on people's hearts and minds to make sure His message would be heard around the world.

Jacques Trémoulet

Two radio pioneers had much to do with what would eventually develop into Adventist World Radio. The backstory first takes us to Jacques Trémoulet. Jacques was born on October 2, 1896, in a little town called Gap, not far from the shores of the Mediterranean Sea, at the foot of the Alps in southern France. While still in his twenties, he became part of the exciting early days of amateur radio. The invention of the wireless radio by Guglielmo Marconi before the turn of the century led to the worldwide explosion of communication via radio waves.

It did not take long before young Trémoulet developed the idea of using radio waves not only to communicate person to person but to broadcast to many people at once. Being adept at mechanical tinkering, he was able, with help from a friend, to build a small radio transmitter that would be one of the first commercial radio stations in France. From that humble beginning, he would become one of the most influential leaders in European radio broadcasting. It was his work that laid the foundation for the Seventh-day Adventist Church to have a voice across Europe and around the world.

In 1925, Trémoulet's first radio station began broadcasting from Toulouse, one of the larger cities of southern France. He called the station Radio Toulouse. It was the first installation on the Continent to broadcast in multiple languages, including French and English. Radio broadcasts, in general, were not yet regulated by state governments. It was a brand-new medium, and its impact on the public was yet to be discovered by national leaders.

The first nationally controlled broadcaster was the British Broadcasting Company, founded in 1922. In Great Britain, the government controlled the airwaves but had difficulty gaining listeners with its bland, official government programming. This gave the upstart private radio broadcasters in France a big target for their English broadcasts.

Trémoulet seized the opportunity to gain not only a large audience but also to bring in funding to support his plans for additional expansion of his radio network. His next project was the acquisition of Radio Bordeaux. His home country announced it would soon begin regulating the growing radio industry, so he started looking for an alternative option in other countries. By 1931, he had found his opportunity in the Grand Duchy of Luxembourg. Within a year, Radio Luxembourg was conducting on-air testing, and in 1933, programs in English were beamed at the British Isles from this most strategically located station.

H. M. S. Richards

At the same time as Trémoulet was expanding his radio empire, there was another radio champion busy within the Seventh-day Adventist Church. That pioneer was H. M. S. Richards Sr., best known as the

Introduction

founder of the *Voice of Prophecy* radio program. Harold Marshall Sylvester Richards was born in 1894 in Davis City, Iowa. As an infant, he nearly died at one point, and his mother promised to dedicate him to the service of God if he survived. That mother's prayer was answered, and from that time on, he was taught that he belonged to God.[1]

Richards gave his first sermon when he was four years old: he described the New Jerusalem and all the fruits that will be found there. For his message, he was given a bowl of oranges that were on the table from which he preached. From then on, he practiced his sermons on his younger brother. As a young man, he became a leader in his Colorado church, where the members appointed him as an elder, the top lay leadership position in Adventist churches.

After graduating from Washington Missionary College in Maryland (now Washington Adventist University) during the World War I era, he held evangelistic meetings in several locations and was identified by church leaders as a dedicated minister. He was soon ordained as a minister of the gospel and later became an evangelist in California.

In 1926, Richards participated in an experimental radio broadcast, and he was hooked. He immediately saw the potential of the medium for sharing the gospel message with the masses. He began broadcasting early morning devotionals over KNX in Los Angeles in 1929, and later, he started a program called *Tabernacle of the Air* on KGER, Long Beach. By 1937, he was on the air with a thirty-minute Sunday evening program on nine stations in California and Arizona. His radio career was well underway.

In 1942, Fordyce Detamore, a returning overseas missionary, joined Richards as an associate director. It was Detamore's idea to create a Bible correspondence school—a concept that Richards would promote worldwide. Thus, the way was prepared for AWR, years later, to have a ready-made follow-up facility for processing the Bible study requests generated from its broadcasts. Richard's crusade to establish Bible schools stretched into Asia and Europe.

In 1949, Detamore was instrumental in getting Richard's half-hour program, by then called the *Voice of Prophecy*, on the airwaves of the American Broadcasting Company's seven hundred stations. At about that same time, the program was launched internationally on Radio Luxembourg.

World War II

After its launch in 1933, the signal from the radio station in Luxembourg was heard clearly all over Great Britain, and soon it was the most popular station in the area. Its programming was sponsored by commercial clients, such as Ovaltine and Horlicks (hot drink manufacturers in Britain), along with other brands. With the incredible success of the Luxembourg station, Trémoulet was encouraged to expand his empire with the purchase of a station in Paris and another in Andorra—a small country snuggled in the mountains between France and Spain. Radio Andorra went on air in the fall of 1939.

His stations were very successful financially, and he was a prime example of a successful businessman, known all over France as a force in society, even as war clouds were gathering across the Continent. The horrors of World War II were about to envelop central Europe.

On May 10, 1940, the German army entered Luxembourg, and Trémoulet's station was confiscated for use as Nazi Germany's main propaganda voice. As enemy forces entered France itself, Trémoulet's other stations were also confiscated for propaganda use. Trémoulet and his family escaped to neutral Spain, where he spent the rest of his life. His only surviving station was Radio Andorra. Like Spain, Andorra declared its neutrality in the war, and that station became its only voice on the airwaves. To keep the station on the air, Trémoulet and his staff decided to make the station programming neutral, just as the country was neutral. Only music and nonpolitical announcements were aired.

When the Americans arrived to liberate Luxembourg in 1944, they wasted no time in commandeering Radio Luxembourg for their own propaganda use. Much of the equipment was damaged, so it took some work to get the station back on the air. When hostilities ended in 1945, the Luxembourg station was returned to Trémoulet's company. It was again a welcome sound across central Europe and the British Isles.

It was during this time that the United States announced the Marshall Plan to help the shattered economies of Europe recover from the turmoil resulting from the war. American agencies, including the Seventh-day Adventist Church, sent emissaries to assist in the implementation of the recovery plan.

This was when Trémoulet met the Adventists.

Introduction

Jacques Trémoulet and Adventist radio

Trémoulet's network in Europe south of the French border was growing. In 1942, he added Radio Monte Carlo.

Upon meeting some Seventh-day Adventists, he discovered they were trying to bring hope, food, and clothing to those suffering from the collapse of Europe's national economies. He was sympathetic to their cause, and after meeting together, the Adventists happily agreed to purchase airtime on his stations, starting with Radio Luxembourg and Radio Monte Carlo. But it took until 1947 for them to realize their plans when *La Voix de l'Espérance*, "The Voice of Hope," went on the air over much of Europe.

In 1951, Radio Luxembourg installed a new medium wave transmitter, and Trémoulet, remembering the Adventists who had taken up his cause at the end of the war, sold time on the station for their English broadcast of the *Voice of Prophecy*.

In 1952, Radio Tangier came on the air with *La Voix de l'Esperance*. The church was carrying out its mission of reaching as many people as possible with the gospel message, following Jesus' instructions: "Go ye into all the world" (Mark 16:15) and "teach all nations" (Matthew 28:19).

The relationship between Trémoulet and the church was cordial and respectful; each had an appreciation for what they could do together. Monsieur Trémoulet felt a deep connection with the Adventist message and appreciated their dependability and financial fidelity—they always paid their bills! Although he never became an official member of the church, he said, "In heart I am an Adventist."[2]

He went on to establish more stations in Spain and one in the Caribbean—Radio Antilles. Meanwhile, in Europe, governments tightened their control of radio frequencies. Nationally controlled stations would not accept certain religious programs on their airwaves. And on most of the Continent, private radio stations were prohibited.

But Trémoulet still wanted to help the Adventists expand their reach and found the opportunity in Portugal in 1969. He was able to sign a thirty-year lease with the government there for one of the most powerful shortwave stations in Western Europe: Radio Trans-Europe. The station's 250-kilowatt transmitters would allow the Adventists to reach all of Europe, North Africa, and the Middle East.

Trémoulet was excited to invite the church to rent time on this new station at a significantly discounted price. He told James Aitken, a church official, he would also give the Adventists first choice of airtime. The offer was very generous. Aitken carried the news back to church headquarters in Washington, DC. He knew he would have an ally for the project in Neal C. Wilson, the president of the Seventh-day Adventist Church in North America. Together they began to promote the idea to church leadership. Robert Pierson, the president of the Seventh-day Adventist world church, was favorable to the idea. But the nagging question was, Where will we get the money?

While this discussion was taking place in Washington, a Scandinavian religious group heard about the new station in Portugal and convinced Trémoulet that he should rent time to them. Weary of waiting for the Adventists to make up their minds, he decided to sell time to the Scandinavian group so the transmitter could begin operating sooner rather than later.

By early 1971, the Adventist leaders had settled on a strategy for broadcasting over Radio Trans-Europe. They would challenge members around the world to join them in the mission of launching programs for the large part of the world that could receive the signal from Portugal. The church headquarters would cover the costs for the first year, but church members would decide with their contributions whether the programs would continue beyond that year. They proposed to launch the broadcasts in faith—"A Bold New Move," they called it—in the belief that church members would be inspired by God to do their part to support the project over the longer term.

With media-savvy radio pastor Roger Fasnacht and his assistant Bernard Pichot in Paris, a program schedule was formulated based on church resources in various countries. Plans called for twelve hours a week on the air in various languages: French, German, Italian, Greek, Croatian, Serbian, Hungarian, Czech, Slovenian, Macedonian, Romanian, Arabic, Russian, Ukrainian, Polish, and English. Nearly all of those language groups already had Bible Correspondence Schools, thanks to years of promotion by H. M. S. Richards. The church was now well positioned to accomplish a great work through God's "Air Force."

---

1. Information in this section has been adapted from Orley M. Berg, "H. M. S. Richards: Committed Evangelist Preacher," *Ministry*, October 1970, 4–7.

2. S. F. Monnier, "A Dream Come True," *Quarterly Review*, June 1971, 3, https://documents.adventistarchives.org/Periodicals/SEQR/SEQR19710601-V38-02.pdf.

ONE

Learning to Live

I was born in Johnson City, near Binghamton, New York, in the midst of the Second World War. Both my parents were descendants of a French Huguenot family that migrated to the New York City area in 1700, a few years after the name of that city was changed from New Amsterdam to New York. My parents, Anna Elizabeth and Kenneth Steele, were both from the line of André Lamoureaux, a Huguenot Protestant. My mother's ancestry follows a direct line to the family patriarch, who fled France because of religious persecution. Her mother's maiden name was Elizabeth Lamoureaux.

André was born in a small inland village in France, where he learned about the teachings of John Huss and John Calvin. In his teens, he left home and traveled to the village of Meschers-sur-Gironde, near La Rochelle on the Atlantic coast, where, under the tutelage of his uncle, he became a pilot guiding foreign cargo ships through the shifting sands of the river Gironde to the major shipping port of Bordeaux. Eventually, he became a ship's captain. In his own small boat, he carried family members and fellow believers to Bristol, England. After a couple of years there, he made the more perilous sea journey in his small ship with family and friends across the Atlantic to New York.

My father's lineage to André was somewhat altered when a Scotsman,

Peter Steele Jr., married a Lamoureaux girl by the name of Charity. Peter was a Scotsman who immigrated from Ireland and jumped ship in Pennsylvania before it reached Philadelphia. The Steele family became farmers and eventually moved north to the Scranton and Wilkes-Barre areas of Pennsylvania. It was there that my grandparents' families, actually their two sons and two daughters, connected. My father married my mother, Anna Elizabeth Garringer, and his brother Ed married her sister, Arlene Garringer.

I do not remember anything about my grandparents. My father and his brothers left home as soon as they were able. My uncles rarely talked about their father, but when they did, it was not complimentary. I got the message that he was a farmer and a difficult man, who was very hard on the children—especially his sons, and they left home under less-than-pleasant circumstances. So, by the time I came along, those grandparents were out of the picture. On the other hand, my mother's parents were greatly beloved, and I was told how Grandmother Garringer used to sit me on her lap and cuddle her newest grandson when I was less than two years old.

My mother's parents were devout Seventh-day Adventists, having accepted the religion after a book salesman came to the door and sold my grandmother a Christian book. Her baptism was recorded in a Scranton newspaper. The headline read, "Adventists Hold Their Solemn Services of Baptism." The event took place on the Susquehanna River, meaning "Muddy Water," so named by the Algonquin American Indians.

"It was but the making of the day when old records were washed away and sought a resting place on the pebble bottom of the famous stream and new pledges and troths were plighted with the Creator," reported the newspaper. The reporter counted several hundred people lining the banks of the river, standing on a bridge, and clumping together in a small fleet of canoes and rowboats. One by one, the eight new believers were led into the chilly waters by a pastor from the Scranton church, who lowered them into the water with the words, "I now baptize you in the name of the Father, the Son, and the Holy Spirit." The last person to enter those cold waters that day was my grandmother, Elizabeth Garringer.

Times must have been hard for my parents when I was born; they already had three kids and were living on a farm in northern

Learning to Live

Pennsylvania, just across from the New York state line. My older siblings tell of harsh winters when my mother ran the farm alone. My father, to keep the family afloat, took a job at a shoe factory in the city—the Endicott-Johnson Shoe Corporation—so he was away most days. He was an essential worker for the war effort because the shoe company was the largest army-boot manufacturer in the country.

In the winter, Dad stayed with relatives in the city and came home on weekends. The circumstances were especially hard on my mom; she was slightly crippled from birth with what she called a clubfoot, which required surgery to insert a metal rod in her leg so she could walk normally. Forever afterward, she struggled with leg and foot discomforts.

Thanks to the generous job benefits at my father's workplace, my parents had saved enough to put a down payment on their own property near a place called Little Meadows. To the delight of my sisters and brother, our farm was within walking distance of a magical summer vacation retreat at Lake O'Meadows, where they could swim and boat on lazy summer days. The lake was surrounded by small white rental cottages where families from the cities came to enjoy summer vacations.

My family became well known to the owners of the resort, who permitted my siblings to have free run of the place. We were so well known that I remember my parents saying they were actually good friends with the owners. It was a friendship that resulted in a gigantic move for our family two years after I was born. My brother, Darrell, became deathly sick during the winter months, and doctors told my parents he might not make it unless they took him to a warmer climate. Our friends who owned the nearby resort, hearing of the problem, made my dad an offer: his farm for a house they owned in St. Petersburg, Florida. The idea of never-ending sunshine made Dad immediately decide to take them up on the deal. In 1945, he packed up the family in his old black Buick and joined the postwar masses of people migrating south and west.

At only two years old, I don't remember that epic trip. But I do remember a subsequent journey when we all piled into that old Buick and traveled back north to visit relatives. To save money and time, my dad decided we would travel through the night. But late in the evening, as we were traveling through open-range country in north Florida, a cow walked right out onto the highway in front of our car.

The crash damaged the radiator and right front fender of the car, and we were stranded in the middle of nowhere in the middle of the night! Traffic was rare at that time of day, but finally, a kind trucker stopped and offered to pull us into the next town so we could find a repair shop. The local mechanic's garage was closed, but the owner and his family sympathized with our plight and invited us to spend the night in their new, unfinished house behind the garage. It offered a roof over our heads, but it had no windows or doors, so we spent a miserable night in mosquito country. The next day, while the car was being repaired, the family offered us a meal of potato salad and deep-fried pigs' tails.

My mom was horrified by the meal. She had been brought up by Adventist parents who knew pork was an unclean food. But she graciously thanked the family because we would certainly enjoy the potato salad and some snacks she had brought along. The mechanic spent a full day beating out the metal on the front fender so it wouldn't scrape the wheel, and by evening, we were again on our way north, headed for the Blue Ridge Parkway in Virginia and through Maryland into familiar scenery—the rolling green hills of Pennsylvania. My dad had to stop frequently to put water in the car's radiator, which had a small leak from the cow accident. I can still picture him catching cold water at a roadside waterfall when we were still on the Blue Ridge Parkway in the Appalachian Mountains. It was a most memorable family travel experience.

When the family had finally settled in Florida, my mom started looking for a church. We kids were soon attending Bible studies and church services at the Adventist church in the Mound Park area of the city. My father thought the church demanded too much of its members, plus he thought he was not good enough to go to church, so it was a one-sided attempt at Christianity, with my mom leading the way the best she could.

Both of my parents had to find work to support the family of four children, with another soon on the way. My mom first got a job as a waitress at a restaurant that made its own potato chips. I remember how amazed I was to visit the shop's kitchen, where I saw the chips frying in a vat of oil. Eventually, my mom met a family in the church who ran a rest home, and through that connection, she became a nurse's aide and later a nurse. My dad temporarily joined a construction crew that was building houses in the booming city of St. Petersburg. Later he was employed for many years as a maintenance supervisor at the Municipal Repair Shop.

Dad was proud to have a permanent job with the city government. He was loyal to the city; years later, when he retired, he was lauded for his long tenure. My main memory of his job was when our family attended the annual Christmas party for city employees. Numerous door prizes were handed out, and my dad always hoped to win a television or radio as a prize. But every time his name was called, he received a big tinned ham. He was disgusted when that happened because he knew my mom would not let him bring "that thing" into our house.

Much to the delight of us kids, the Gulf of Mexico's beaches were a short drive away, and we often joined other young people from church for an evening at the beach. We could roast vegetarian hot dogs over a small fire in the sand, followed by roasted marshmallows. Even with the austerity at home, we thought life was good.

Not long after our arrival in Florida, my baby brother, Lanny, was born. I remember well the night Mom was taken to the hospital for the delivery. It was in the middle of a hurricane. The storm was slashing telephone poles and blowing down trees onto the streets. My dad became the hero of the family for dodging all the obstacles to get my mom to the hospital in time for the delivery. We kids were enamored with our new brother. Lanny and I became playmates once he was old enough for me to boss him around.

When I was six years old, our church opened a school in a downtown neighborhood—a house on a corner residential lot had been converted into a two-room school. Two teachers taught grades one through eight, half in one room and half in the other larger room. My mom desperately wanted us to be students in that school, so she took on a second nursing job to afford our tuition. That meant she was away from home for most of each day. And when she was at home, she was extremely tired and needed rest. It was about this time that she was diagnosed with diabetes, and her life got even busier with insulin, needles, and stress.

To get to school, we had to ride a city bus that had a stop just one house away from where we lived. One of my early heroes was the bus driver, whose name was Lottie. Every morning we greeted her as an old friend. A disappointing aspect about the bus ride to school was that I was not permitted to sit in the back seat. For some reason, I thought it would be fun to be in the back, where I could observe all the people getting on and off the bus. But a sign over the back row read, "Rear seat reserved for colored." As a first-grader, I couldn't understand why those people merited reserved seats. I was too young to understand the meaning of segregation.

The bus route on Fifteenth Avenue South marked the dividing line between whites and blacks in the city. South of that line lived the whites, including the first block where we lived. In search of playmates, I made friends with some of the black children in the first house on the other side of the street. We played hide-and-seek in the palmetto scrub. Occasionally, I would end up on the back steps of their house, where I sat and watched the chickens pecking the black dirt for anything edible.

My older sisters, Elsie and Eileen, became after-school babysitters for Lanny and me. I resented my mom's absence, so I took it out on my sisters by cooperating as little as possible. Even so, they accepted the responsibility, and my memories of those days are mainly of their attempts to keep me in line and their efforts to invent meals that Lanny and I would eat. Later they both left home to attend the church's boarding high school in a distant city.

My older brother, Darrell, continued to live at home but had an especially hard time adjusting to public school. He preferred his teen friends from church, for which my mom was thankful, but it seemed even with those friends, he was always getting into trouble. His high jinks became legendary as he roamed the city with his buddies, and they got into trouble with neighbors and were noted on a police watch list. My dad was at his wit's end to know what to do. Shouting arguments between the two became common.

I remember the day when Darrell decided to leave home. He didn't tell Dad he was leaving, but somehow Mother found out, probably from my older sister. Mom knew there was nothing she could do to stop him from going, so she made lunches for him and his friend, prayed with them, and sent them on their way with all the money she had in her purse. Eventually, he sent a letter home saying he got a job on a ranch out west. I was jealous—my greatest desire was to be a cowboy too. In later years, I left on an overseas mission for the church, and eventually, my brother became an ardent promoter of missions and helped build schools and churches in Central and South America.

When I was in the third grade, the church bought a property about ten blocks from our house for a new three-room schoolhouse. Lanny and I were soon enrolled. The first two years of high school were also offered there, so I eventually moved to the upper-grade classroom. My mom was still working two jobs, but with the school so close, we could walk, putting less of a financial burden on my parents. Our walk to school was about five blocks through our neighborhood to the Atlantic Seaboard railroad tracks. We then walked the tracks for about three blocks, over a railroad trestle, and around a small lake to get to school.

The wooded area along the tracks was a great adventure playground for neighborhood kids. But the vacant lands were full of rattlesnakes, so we had to learn how to avoid them: walk quietly, keep an eye out, and don't be the last one in line when you were walking through the palmettos because the snakes would always strike the last person, or so we believed. And at the shores of the lake were more poisonous snakes—copperheads. Sometimes we would see the beady eyes of an alligator in the lake.

One day when I was in the ninth grade, our teacher discovered the lone alligator in the lake had died, probably of old age, and was lying just across the field from our school. So we had a biology class in the open air as he dissected the seven-foot gator and pulled out its inner organs with his hands. He found its heart, liver, and other organs, which he eagerly displayed before our wavering eyes.

It was in these teen years that I gained new confidence. The financial struggles of my parents to pay the private school's tuition were well known by church leaders, so the school board chair offered me a summer job, painting and cleaning around the school. Later a kind church member, a master electrician, got me a job as a helper at his company, so I spent numerous summer days pulling electrical wires through fiberglass-filled attics or squirming among spiderwebs and scorpion nests under the floors of wooden houses. My mother contributed what she could for our tuition, but these jobs and generous donations by church members kept us in the private Adventist school.

Many years later, when I became a member of school boards myself, I remembered the kindness of those generous people. It was that kind of sacrifice that got me through eighteen years of Christian education. I forever afterward have been a champion for Adventist Christian education.

Two

Finding Myself

I've often wondered how children intuitively demonstrate at a young age what they will do in adult life. I've heard music prodigies tell how they naturally started reacting to music as an infant and how that became a talent that followed them through childhood, youth, and adulthood. In my own extended family, I've witnessed how kids can instinctively latch on to sporting activities, starting with acrobatic tricks as toddlers, and then continue to hone their physical activities until they enter organized sports at school.

There must be other traits that manifest themselves shortly after birth that indicate what talents one will have in adult life. Will a toddler who is good at numbers become an accountant? Or will a toddler who tends to organize all his toys and personal belongings become a business manager? Or will a little girl who is inordinately interested in dressing a doll in beautiful clothes become a clothing designer?

From my earliest memories, I remember I was always fascinated by machines that produced music. How could a radio box, squat and square, send out a sound that caused human beings to react, usually in very positive ways? The music, I noticed, caused adults to relax and sometimes even burst out in song themselves. My father was in his most pleasant mood when he was listening to music on his car radio.

Finding Myself

I liked what music could do for people. Eventually, I began to notice that someone was speaking in between the music segments, saying things that helped people to understand the music. This gave a sense of well-being to those who were listening. It seemed that a good friend was taking people through their work, everyday activities, and lives. I thought, *My, that is a nice thing to do—have a friend who knows what you want to hear and share with you the lonely as well as happy times.*

When I was nine years old, I received a couple of Disney records for my birthday. My parents also had purchased a dark-red Airline record player from Montgomery Ward, and with that and my records, I became a junior disc jockey. I learned how to time my music and my announcements so that they came together as a radio program should—seamlessly. My main problem was finding an audience. The only one around was my five-year-old brother Lanny, so I was constantly insisting that he sit and listen to my radio program. It was not easy, of course, for he had his own things he wanted to do.

Often, as I was about to introduce the next tune on my show, I would notice my audience glancing from side to side, looking for an escape route. "Oh no, you don't," I threatened. "You can wait just a few more minutes till the end of my show! Now stay here." When Lanny's face began to pucker into a wild yell for Mama, I knew I had lost my audience.

He taught me my first lesson in broadcasting: your audience has an attention span of only a few minutes. In broadcasting, we remind ourselves of that fact with the acronym KISS: Keep it short, stupid! If your program is too long, you'll lose your audience. And I guess that was my earliest lesson in communication and the earliest indication of how I might spend my adult life.

When it was time for me to enter my last two years of high school, my mother thought I would naturally want to attend the same boarding high school in upstate Florida as my sisters. But I wanted something different, so I begged to attend Fletcher Academy in North Carolina. I argued that I'd had enough of the flat Florida landscape. The mountains of western North Carolina beckoned.

My sisters, by then, had finished high school, returned home for a brief time, and were dreaming of finding jobs in Atlanta, where both would soon find husbands. They met their spouses while attending church in the city. My older brother, Darrell, had finished his cowboy days in the West and was back in Florida, staying with my parents, and was now a member of a fishing boat crew. But my time for launching out, more or less on my own, had come.

I must have been persuasive because my mother finally gave me permission to apply to the school in North Carolina. It probably helped her to know that Bill Wilson, my sister's new brother-in-law, was the administrator of the school and the hospital that was connected to it on campus. He and his wife, Beverly, were now part of our extended family.

"School of the Mountains" goes the school song. With fewer than two hundred students, Fletcher Academy is a school where parents hope their teenage child will learn not only scholastic and social skills but also to love God. All of that was what I needed and what I got.

Classes were well taught, the food was good, my friends were many, and my work skills were sharpened. My parents still had difficulty paying my tuition, so I worked at the school farm and the nearby hospital to help pay the bills. I went to campus early to pick up a summer job working in the school gardens, picking tomatoes, pulling carrots, and weeding the growing plants. The produce went to the school kitchen and was served to us in the cafeteria.

When school started that fall, I was invited by the dean to be the dormitory monitor. It was my job every morning to knock loudly on doors to wake the boys in time for our morning devotional in the worship room. There faculty and others would share devotional thoughts and pray that God would guide us through our busy days.

One of the most interesting men who came to lead our devotionals was Mr. Beadle. We boys thought his name was fascinating but so were his devotional thoughts. They were usually based on stories from *Reader's Digest*. He would read the stories to us, then use them to draw a spiritual application. After morning worship, we hit the cafeteria for breakfast, hurried off to classes, returned for lunch, ran back to classes, and then back to the cafeteria for supper. Naturally, the meals were the biggest social event of the day.

Evenings were supposed to be study time unless you were part of the school choir or band. In those cases, rehearsals were required. I joined both the choir and the band and "pretended" to play the trombone. For me, rehearsals meant acting like I knew what I was doing and faking it a lot. My memories of my band and choir directors were their contorted faces as they heard the strange sounds I made.

I never really mastered that horn, but I did learn to sing and, in my senior year, was elected president of the school choir. The top benefit of being in one of the music organizations was the band and choir trips off campus. The band didn't travel much, but the choir frequently went to sing in Adventist churches in surrounding cities. We became the school's main point of contact with potential donors and students. We students found the trips very helpful in cementing friendships. As members of this elite group, we could choose whom we sat by when we traveled. I think back on those days and remember a number of couples that formed lasting relationships and marriages as a result of those choir trips.

When I was ready to enter college, my mom revealed a secret she had kept for years: when I was born, she was told by the doctor that her child might not make it. I was a "blue baby," struggling with a respiratory condition. That night in her hospital bed, she prayed and promised God that if He would permit me to live, she would dedicate me to His work. I was not happy to hear her secret. I saw myself as a future business administrator, so I signed up for a bachelor's degree in business at Southern Missionary College (now Southern Adventist University).

Late in my first semester, it became clear that my talents were not in accounting or economics. My academic advisor informed me I was not making grades high enough to stay in the business program. I was thrown into crisis mode. At the time, I volunteered as an announcer on WSMC—the little 10-watt radio station owned by the university. I was having fun reading news bulletins and spinning records for the benefit of the few listeners we had in the little valley of Collegedale, Tennessee. It was then that God opened my eyes: I realized that a communication degree was my future. I soon accepted a management position at the station and ended my senior year as the station manager.

As the manager, I felt impressed that our little station could have a larger outreach if we could find a higher elevation for our antenna and raise the wattage to reach over the mountain into the city of Chattanooga. The chair of the Religion Department was enthusiastic about the idea. The project was set, and within a year, we were offered a mountaintop site for our tower and enough money to purchase a 50,000-watt transmitter! WSMC became a big-time station! It made me realize that God likes to see us think big for Him so He can make big things happen!

Another event that inspired my future was a visit to campus by the veteran Adventist broadcast evangelist, H. M. S. Richards Sr. He was a hero to the communication majors, and he promoted the concept of radio as a way to evangelize the world! "With just one or two powerful radio stations, we can reach the whole world," he said. That thought entered my brain and teased me for years. Thanks to him, my compass was set.

After graduation, I traveled to Memphis, Tennessee, planning to enter a graduate program in broadcasting at a state university. It was several months before the academic year was to begin, so I searched for a job and was employed as a cameraman at WKNO-TV, the public broadcasting station in the city. I missed the intimacy of radio but was happy to learn about television operations.

A month before classes were to begin, a letter arrived. It was from "Uncle Sam"—the US Government. I was notified that I was being called up for military service. My hometown Selective Service office permitted me to finish my college degree, but their policy then called for me to give two years of service to my country. As an Adventist, I was inducted into the army as a noncombatant. But after my basic training and four weeks into advanced individual training as a medical corpsman, the unit personnel officer discovered he had a television cameraman on his hands and drafted orders to transfer me to the US Army Infantry Training School at Fort Benning, Georgia.

"Get a mop, and mop the studio floor," my sergeant ordered. It was my first assignment in the "spit and polish" television division at the training school. It became a recurring routine, and I quickly became disillusioned with television work. Occasionally, we would take our cameras and mobile production studio into the field, but I longed for the immediacy of a radio microphone.

"Well, I don't know if you deserve it or not," Sergeant Brown said lackadaisically, "but I have a notice here that you are being sent to Europe!"

I could hardly believe it! Just when I was at my lowest in the US Army, the Lord came along and arranged a free trip to Europe! What did He have in mind?

"I believe I deserve it, Sergeant," I said politely and took the orders from his hands.

"Good luck to you," he said.

Finding Myself

Within two weeks, I was on a troop charter plane headed out over the Atlantic to Frankfurt, Germany. I had no idea it was the same trip I would make again years later when I joined God's "Air Force"!

My time in Germany started with a bang. About twelve of us soldiers were marching down a main street in Frankfurt on our way to the *Hauptbahnhof* (central train station), walking in single file; each one followed the one in front of him, carrying our huge duffel bags, full of our earthly possessions over our shoulders. A large black Mercedes-Benz came up beside us, and a woman yelled out the window, "Hurrah for the US Army!" The soldier in the lead was so distracted by the woman's yell that he walked straight into a telephone pole. It started a chain reaction, and we all stumbled and fell like dominoes! What a graceful way to enter Germany!

I was stationed in the town of Hanau to serve as a clerk in the 574th Personnel Services Company. The 574th was the personnel headquarters for the army in Europe. New recruits with college degrees were automatically assigned to this company to serve as personnel records clerks.

I was keen to attend Sabbath church services and discovered that a short train ride back to the city of Frankfurt would take me to the Seventh-day Adventist Servicemen's Center. It was a large converted house on a side street downtown that provided weekend accommodation for service members at no cost. My problem was that I needed to get permission from my commanding officer (CO) to leave my post on Saturdays.

"Sir, I'm a Seventh-day Adventist, and I request permission to attend services at my church on Saturdays. I am willing to work Sundays to compensate for my absence on Saturdays." (This was a request I would need to repeat several times—whenever our company got a new CO. Those visits to our new commanders were, by far, the most stressful moments of my life there.)

After many prayers, I got the courage to make an appointment to appear before the company's CO. With my legs shaking and my heart pounding, I was surprised by his response: "And what do Seventh-day Adventists believe?" I couldn't believe it. God had created this opportunity for me to witness to my CO! He thanked me for the information about Adventists and said he had no problem with me being absent on Saturdays, so long as I was willing to take Sunday duty.

My time in Europe at Uncle Sam's expense gave me the opportunity to travel to most of the countries on the Continent. I observed life from Sweden in the north to Spain in the south and from Germany to Great Britain. I even made side trips to Communist East Berlin and Libya in North Africa. My goal was to experience as much as possible because I feared I might never return to this great cradle of civilization. How little did I know!

Three

Three Loves

"Well, where do you want to go in the USA?" asked the army transportation clerk. Having completed my tour of duty, I was completely free—for the first time—to decide my next direction in life. After thinking over my options, I decided that if I really wanted to pursue my dream of working in Adventist radio, I should see what I could find in Washington, DC, which is home to the Seventh-day Adventist Church's world headquarters. It also seemed an ideal place for finding some good Christian friends. I knew the city had several Adventist churches, a college, and a few hospitals. All this, plus the excitement of life in the nation's capital.

"Washington, DC," I replied with only a slight hesitation. The next day I had my ticket to Washington.

I arrived there with no friends, no contacts, and no home. But God soon saw that I had them all! My goal was to find a job in Adventist radio, if possible, and to get involved in church youth activities. Fortunately, I had my discharge allowance from the military, so I had the funds to survive for several months. I found an apartment near Columbia Union College (now Washington Adventist University) and started checking out the churches and jobs in the area.

Radio jobs were scarce, so that line of work would have to wait. I applied for a job at Leland Memorial Hospital and was accepted as an assistant in the personnel department. My main responsibilities were interviewing job applicants and keeping the personnel records in order.

"Would you be interested in leading out in our public relations projects?" the hospital administrator asked me a few months after I began work. As the public relations director, I soon was arranging health displays, organizing smoking-cessation clinics, and editing a health journal for the hospital foundation.

I couldn't give up my love for radio work, so I sought ways to connect with the church headquarters to see whether I could volunteer to make radio programs. I had friends at several Adventist radio stations, who had organized the Adventist Radio Network (ARN), and I thought the stations might be interested in programs from the church headquarters in Washington. I proposed the idea of a weekly press conference. "We might even be able to get a weekly program by the church president," I told the ARN managers. "Let's go for it," came back the reply from ARN President Don Dick. "I think the stations will be very interested."

Our first radio program from the church headquarters was the *Adventist Press Conference*. I invited staff from several offices at the General Conference, where there were reporters or writers, to come to a weekly recording of the press conference with various church officials. My team consisted of Rosie Bradley from the *Review and Herald* magazine; Pat Horning and Chuck Scriven from the youth magazine, *Insight*; and Kit Watts from the Sligo Seventh-day Adventist Church staff.

Next, I began working on a strategy to convince the church president, Robert Pierson, to consider recording a weekly program. "I'm intrigued by the concept of having regular communication with the public," he said. "My main problem is finding the time to do the recordings." Here was an opening with the busiest man at the world headquarters.

Five days later, he called me back. "I've been thinking it over, and I definitely want to do this. Only one thing: the only time I can do it is first thing in the morning, before office hours. Is that possible?"

"Of course," I said, wondering how I would manage to get in a recording session before I traveled to the hospital to start my day of work. Where there's a will, there's a way, and soon we were in the routine of meeting once a week at 6 A.M. for the recording session of his program, which he chose to call *Let's Talk It Over*. For me, that morning rendezvous with the president was like my morning devotional.

Three Loves

One day I was sitting in the little windowless room that served as our recording studio in the South Building of the church office complex when a strange thing happened. The studio was sparsely furnished with a gray table, two gray chairs, and a small portable recorder on which I did the recording and editing. I was concentrating on editing the tape—marking, cutting, and then splicing the recorded magnetic tape.

Suddenly, I felt a pull on the tape in my left hand, and the pulling continued. Something was "eating" *Let's Talk It Over*! I had to find out what was chewing up my precious recording, so I followed the tape down the side of the desk and watched the tape as it was pulled steadily into the wall heater! The heater's fan had caught the end of the tape in its draft and was slowly winding it around the fan shaft. A whole program had to be recorded again; I sheepishly informed the president the next day.

I was back in radio and loving it. I was also enjoying the fellowship of the vibrant church community in the capital. Sensing a need to serve the church even more, I decided to try a new idea out on some of the young people my age. My idea was to form a team of senior young people who would present the Bible study hour and church service at smaller churches in the region on Sabbaths. Soon we had a group of about ten independent young singles committed to joining.

At the organization meeting, I marveled at the talent we had pulled together. There were musicians, teachers, editors, medical specialists, media specialists, an aspiring lawyer, and other young professionals. We named our group the "Wider Circle"—a name taken from a poem or book one of the group members had recently read. In no time, our church-service strategy was clear: different members of the group would assume the personalities of various Bible characters in the New Testament whose lives were changed when they met Jesus. The personal experiences of Mary and Martha, the rich young ruler, the apostles, and blind Bartimaeus had the audience enthralled. It was a great success, and the group continued even after I left the area two years later.

One night we had a Wider Circle practice session, and in came a new young woman named Andrea Grover. I remember welcoming her to the group and thinking nothing special about our meeting until eight days later.

While sitting at my office desk at the hospital, I picked up the newsletter from the Washington Adventist Hospital across town. I noticed a photo of the new secretary to the public relations director on the back page. Lightning struck. It was that same young woman who had attended our Wider Circle meeting the previous week! She was beautiful! What was I waiting for? I dropped everything and drove to the big hospital in Takoma Park, Maryland.

"I didn't see you at the Wider Circle meeting this week and was wondering what you think of our group." It was the best opening I could think of for what I hoped would be a little conversation leading to a date.

"I think it has a lot of potential," she replied. I took that to mean that she thought it was great. Only years later did she confess that she really wasn't so sure the group would have any success. She said she probably would not have come again if I had not encouraged her to return.

It was soon clear that I had found my third love. The first was my love for God. The second was this charming, lively young woman. The third was radio. I had no idea at the time that my three loves would become as compatible as they have, but through the years, Andrea and I discovered that the Lord had a special work for both of us to do.

"It looks like the church may finally be able to use radio to reach all of Europe," James Aitken, the secretary of the church's Radio and Television Department, excitedly said as he leaned over his office desk. "An old friend of the church, Mr. Trémoulet, has been able to get permission from the Portuguese government to install a shortwave transmitter, and he wants to sell airtime to us. He appreciated the help our church gave him and his family after World War II, and now he wants to help us by putting our programs on the air over his own Radio Trans-Europe. If we move fast enough, we will have our choice of airtime."

"Praise the Lord, this is wonderful news," I said, trying to sound as supportive as possible without revealing my excitement about the potential for my own involvement. The Lord made me say, "If you need someone to go over there, I'm certainly available."

"That's precisely why I called you here today, Allen." He looked me straight in the eye. "We're wondering if you would be willing to get this project started over in Lisbon. Your experience in radio and exposure to Europe uniquely qualify you for this job. Would you be interested?"

It was the invitation I had been longing and praying for—my dream job. I wanted to say, "Here am I, send me," but all I could say was, "Indeed, I would be interested." Fearing I didn't appear enthusiastic enough, I added, "When do we start?"

Three Loves

He looked at some papers on his desk and thought out loud. "Well, let's see. The station has promised us our choice of airtime if we are the first to sign up as partners in this project. So I hope we can sign the contract early next year or, at the latest, by spring. It is now December, so we would most likely need you over there by summer. Yes, let's start working on a summer start-up."

Mr. Trémoulet's schedule was far in advance of ours, and I knew I would have to work fast on a special personal item if I hoped to meet that summer deadline.

I had already invited Andrea to meet my family in Florida over the Christmas holidays. I knew then that it would be more than a visit; I had something specific in mind.

"Will you marry me?" I spoke those words on a moonlit night under the stars in my father's little orange grove in Fort Ogden, Florida, near the Peace River. Afterward, he named that stand of trees "Honeymoon Grove" in our honor. Our wedding was set for the last Sunday in May 1971.

The New Year was a glorious one. Back in Washington, that spring's cherry blossoms were like mountains of lace around the reflecting pool downtown, and the Maryland suburbs where we lived were graced by mounds of azaleas. Our wedding day was only a few weeks before our planned departure for Europe.

We included our Wider Circle friends in the wedding service to serve as musicians and read our favorite Bible texts. To avoid the usual wedding pranks that sometimes accompany American weddings, such as "Just Married" signs painted on the groom's car and the tying of old shoes and cans to the rear bumper, I parked my car in Rock Creek Park near a footbridge opposite the Capital Memorial Church of Seventh-day Adventists. After the reception, my best man, my brother Lanny, took us in his car the few blocks to the little bridge, where we crossed over by foot and jumped into my car for a clean getaway.

During the spring and early summer, we looked for books about Portugal. We tried to learn everything we could about the great adventure we were about to begin for the church. We discovered that many Americans did not even know that Portugal was in Europe. "Portugal—isn't that near Panama?"

A debate sprang up about what the new radio enterprise in Europe should be called. Some thought it should be the *Voice of Prophecy* or the *Voice of Hope*—program names already in use by Adventist broadcasters in the Americas and Europe. Adrian Peterson, an Australian pastor in southern Asia, was promoting the name *Adventist World Radio*. Adrian became the most knowledgeable shortwave expert and tireless promoter of AWR, especially among the already existing crowd of shortwave listeners called DXers. The term *DX* stands for "distance unknown," and we discovered that it was such a popular hobby that DX clubs already existed in most countries around the world.

Walter Scragg, the assistant secretary of the Radio and Television Department, was working through the decision-making process of choosing a program name. He was a fascinating New Zealander who possessed a most delicate sensitivity about the meaning of words. It made me feel valued when he asked what I thought the multilanguage programs should be called. I told him I thought we should be totally upfront about who we are, so I favored the name *Adventist World Radio*. "Then let's call it Adventist World Radio," he said. "It has a certain ring, and I think it will wear well."

Walter was our mentor in the radio ministry, our main advocate at church headquarters, and later, a major force behind AWR's most expansive years as its president from 1991 to 1995. We immediately appreciated the sense of value he gave us as part of the church's radio team. He warned us that the church only had enough money to keep us in Portugal for one year, "Do you still want to go?"

"Of course!" said this adventurous young recruit.

One day I was passing by Pastor Aitken's office when I heard his voice speaking louder than I had ever heard before. He was on an overseas telephone call. "Yes, he is coming, and you will take him in as one of your own," he said. A few minutes of silence followed, then, "Yes, you have people who can do it, I'm sure, but we are sending him, and we are funding him." Suddenly, I realized I was the subject of the conversation. I never asked him about what I heard, but obviously, there was some question about the church sending an American to a place where qualified Europeans could easily do the job.

Pat and Kit, two of our Wider Circle friends, came to record our frantic preparations for the trip to Europe. While Pat was busy digging out of us all the information she could about the radio project, Kit was trying every angle for photos. She was on the bed, on top of the dresser, and in our faces as they watched our hectic packing. "Slippers in the salad bowl, that should work," Andrea was quoted as saying in an article in *Insight*, the church's weekly magazine for young adults. We packed dozens of wedding gifts in a big box that would go into storage to await our return to the United States. We didn't know it at the time, but it would be five years before we would see those gifts again.

A few weeks later, *Insight* published the article "Radio Project: Allen and Andrea Leave for Lisbon." In the same issue was a news brief about Mary Ellen Irwin, the wife of Apollo 15 astronaut Jim Irwin. She missed seeing part of her husband's moonwalk, the article reported, because she was busy teaching a Bible study class in one of the Seventh-day Adventist Churches near Nassau Bay, Texas. When asked why she didn't watch her husband's first steps on the moon, she said, "Jim is committed to his mission, and I am committed to mine."[1]

Her statement made me realize the importance of our own mission. We were leaving a very comfortable lifestyle and all of our friends for a pioneering work, and we had no idea what was ahead of us, what loneliness we would feel, or how we would cope in another culture. "Dear God," I prayed, "give us the wisdom and the strength."

As we headed for the airport, I was surprised to see Andrea carrying a large square Tupperware container filled with books. "We forgot to mail these with the other stuff," she said sheepishly, "and I know we're going to need them." I would come to realize that she is the most voracious reader I have ever met. Yes, we would definitely need those books!

While I was adventurous enough to move easily to a new place when necessary, she had a harder time leaving. She lost her father in an automobile accident when she was nine years old, and her mother died just seven years before I met her. She found support and stability in Washington by adopting the Torsten Lundstrom family as her own. Dr. Lundstrom agreed to escort her down the aisle at our wedding as a stand-in father. Now she was leaving to go on a faraway mission with her new husband—a man she was still getting to know.

"I think becoming a missionary is not so much the difficulty of going to a foreign land," she confided as she slipped her hand into mine on board the airplane. "The hard thing about being a missionary is being separated from family and friends." Her tears punctuated her point.

---

1. "Irwin's Wife Misses Moonwalk to Teach Adventist Classes," *Review and Herald*, September 16, 1971, 3.

Four

On the Air

"What a beautiful city you have," I said to Antonio Baiao, the local church conference president, as we looked over the seven hills of Lisbon from a park located on a high point west of the city. We were thoroughly entranced by the colorful city sitting on the estuary where the Tagus River empties into the Atlantic. Lisbon quickly became my favorite city in Europe and remains at the top of my list of favorite cities today.

"Houses and apartments for rent are easy to spot," he said as he drove us around the city to check out the various suburbs. "Owners place little square pieces of paper in the middle of every window."

He took us to the Belém (Bethlehem) section of town to see some apartments that were advertised in the newspaper. When we stepped out of the car at one location, we were immediately surrounded by four ragtag children begging for money. All four were dirty with unkempt hair. One little boy, about three years old, was wearing only a T-shirt; a little girl about the same age was wearing only some underpants.

"Don't give them anything," the building's *porteira* (manager) called out the window. "If you do, they will never stop pestering you," she added as she ushered us into the apartment building. In time, we found out that porteiras are very important people in Portuguese life. They manage the apartment buildings and usually live on the ground floor, where they can keep an eye on everything, including your car. If you tipped the porteira well at Christmastime, you could be sure that everything you owned would be kept under protective surveillance.

We found the one-bedroom apartment to be clean and well furnished. But its greatest asset was the view from the back balcony. From there, we could see the waters of the Tagus River estuary, and at the water's edge was an ornate but delicate building that looked like a small tower. The porteira explained through our interpreter that it was the Belém Tower which, centuries ago, had served as the tollhouse for ships entering and leaving Lisbon's harbor.

Partial view of shortwave antennas at Sines, Portugal, used by Adventist World Radio for its first broadcasts to Europe, North Africa, and the Middle East, 1971.

Just two blocks away were two equally important landmarks: the Jerónimos Monastery and the Monument to the Discoveries, commemorating Portugal as one of the world's leading nations of exploration, resulting in territories on three continents. The monument has statues of the nation's famous explorers, including Vasco da Gama, all lined up on the prow of a ship headed by Prince Henry the Navigator.

We signed the contract for the apartment. It turned out to be the first of three that we inhabited over the years we lived in Lisbon. Soon after we settled into our apartment in Belém, a bumper-car amusement park was set up in the vacant lot behind our building. It became the bane of our existence. It opened for business around midday every Saturday and operated until two the next morning. Our bedroom window opened toward the area. The kids who came to drive the little cars were noisy enough, but the constant blaring of American pop music was worse. The operator apparently had a special affinity for

The author stands before the giant 250 kW transmitters used by Radio Trans-Europe, Sines, Portugal, 1971.

a song called "Mammy Blue." It was almost the only music played after midnight.

"I can take it no longer," I announced to Andrea one Sunday morning. "We have to move if I am going to keep my sanity." So we started searching around town for those small squares of paper in the windows. We were enchanted by the oldest section of town, the Alfama, near the hilltop Castle of Saint George. It had narrow, winding cobblestone sidewalks and streets that sloped up to the top of the hill. (This ancient area was the subject of most of the picture postcards sold in tourist shops.) Above the steep and winding walkways, wet, dripping clothes were hung out to dry on clotheslines that were accessed by pulleys attached within reach of the overhanging balconies. Pedestrians walking below often found themselves anointed with drops of water from above.

It was in this neighborhood that we noticed an apartment for rent, right on the *eléctrico* (streetcar) line on *Rua Voz de Operário* (Voice of the Workers Street) and across from the Church of São Vincente. What fun, we thought, to be in the ancient Alfama Quarter. Here we could get a taste of ancient Lisbon.

Unfortunately, we hadn't bothered to visit the place on a Saturday. If we had, we would have discovered that our new neighborhood was the noisiest place in the city on Saturdays. The largest flea market in the city ended—or started, depending on which way you were going—right in front of our apartment building! Here, a merchant parked his truck every week, set up his microphone and loudspeakers, and hawked woolen blankets all day long.

Sabbath, our one day of rest each week, gave us headaches. For this reason, among others, we decided to start scouting for a third location. This time we headed for a newer part of the city, Benfica, which is renowned in Europe for its championship soccer team. Here we found a place overlooking the Monsanto Forest Park, near a Metro subway stop and only four blocks from the Lisbon Zoo. The zoo had a magnificent variety of animals due to Portugal's vast overseas territories: Angola, Mozambique, and Macao. I enjoyed telling my friends about waking in the middle of the night to the sound of a lion's roar. This became our favorite home, and we were very comfortable there until we left Portugal.

But having settled in our first home, the Belém apartment, we quickly turned our attention to the work of AWR. As part of the agreement with Radio Trans-Europe, we were allocated an office in a suite leased by the station owner. Our office was on the top floor of an eight-story residential building constructed around 1900. The building stood on a busy four-lane thoroughfare, *Rua Braamcamp*, which is one of seven wheel-spoke roads leading into a downtown green called the Eduardo VII Park. At the forefront of the park is a statue of the Marquis of Pombal, who was prime minister at the time of the disastrous earthquake of 1755, which nearly leveled the city. He is credited with galvanizing the shocked people and leading them in rebuilding the city. As a result, he is one of the most venerated statesmen of all time in Portugal.

In the center of our building was something we had never seen before: an open elevator shaft with an ancient, windowed elevator car resembling a cage suspended by cables. A winding stairwell surrounded the contraption. The elevator only held three people, maybe four if necessary. The real joy of riding in the elevator cage was that we could watch each floor pass as we ascended. Sometimes, if the elevator was full, rather than waiting for the cage to slowly ascend and then descend again, I would run up the stairway. If I ran fast enough, I could wave at the people in the elevator on each floor and reach our office on the top floor before the elevator arrived.

Our office was simply furnished but comfortable. The building, being a converted family residence, had two of the bedrooms in the apartment turned into radio studios. One was assigned to AWR. Our office was down the hall in the former kitchen. A single bare lightbulb hung from the center of the ceiling by a chain. There was a small adjacent room, actually the former kitchen pantry, that we used as a storage closet for our radio program library. It was in this environment that we would spend eight hours or more a day. This was our workplace and AWR's first headquarters.

We soon discovered that the station owner rarely came to Lisbon. We learned that Jacques Trémoulet, the Radio Trans-Europe station owner, had passed away just a few months before we arrived in Lisbon. The new owner was his son-in-law Guy Comminges. He left the Lisbon office in the charge of Madam Branca, a very capable, no-nonsense administrative secretary. Even though she appeared to be stern at first, she became a delightful part of our lives. She always gave us good advice and was the final word on anything to do with office decorum or policy. She was also a good guardian of the front door to the office suite—she was our first line of defense for anyone who might visit.

One day, however, I was the only person in the office when I heard the doorbell ring and ring and ring again. Finally, I ran down the hall to see who was at the door. Two parents with three golden-haired children were waiting at the door. They explained they were from Sweden and were looking for the director of programs for the Pentecostal team who occupied the office next to ours. I was busy trying to meet a program deadline, and the only thing I could think of to help them was to show them to the office down the hall. I assumed they would sit and await the arrival of their friends. I then went back to work in the production studio.

The next morning Madam Branca came storming into our office. "Did you invite those people into the office?" she demanded.

"What people?" I replied, searching my mind to figure out who she was talking about. Then, all of a sudden, I remembered the Swedish family from the day before.

"Do you realize they spent the whole night in that office?" she retorted. "You must never let people come into any office unless staff is here," she scolded, then turned and stormed out. Embarrassed, I returned to my work.

Our studios in Paris, France, and Darmstadt, Germany, were the main production centers for our programs. Other studios were established before long in Italy and Greece. The programs were recorded on magnetic tape on ten-inch reels. It was my task to time each program and add station identification announcements and fill music as needed to meet the radio station's exact timing requirements. Then I delivered the tapes to the radio station's on-air studio, located near the little coastal town of Sesimbra, about twenty-five miles south of Lisbon.

Our first day on air was scheduled for October 1, 1971. With that date just a few weeks away, it would be a short time to prepare the first week of programs. Our producers from Paris were coming down to observe the event. They planned to bring several boxes of programs that would air for a couple of months.

Our delivery system to Sesimbra was hardly sophisticated. The Scandinavians working in the office next door delivered their programs in boxes that fit snugly into white grocery bags from a local supermarket. To help the technicians differentiate our programs from theirs, we decided to use yellow bags we collected from a competing chain of supermarkets.

"Someday you ought to write a book about AWR and call it 'A Thousand Yellow Plastic Bags,' " Andrea quipped one day.

"Well, I hope I can come up with a little better title than that," I replied with a chuckle.

Roger Fasnacht and Bernard Pichot arrived from Paris with a carload of pretaped programs. They wanted to witness this great moment for Adventist radio—one that they had been

Pastor Heinz Hopf, *right*, from Germany, delivers the first German language programs to Allen Steele in Lisbon, 1971.

anticipating for months. Their studio was a hub for recording programs in several languages. They even traveled to Yugoslavia (present-day Croatia) to remotely record programs in Eastern European languages.

All our activities centered on the October 1 deadline. It was on our minds continuously, but the day before, it looked like we might not make it. I worked on the programs for most of the night of September 30, and finally, after only a couple of hours of sleep, I was ready to dash down to Sesimbra with the first programs. We arrived just minutes before the first broadcast. The technicians were waiting at the door and quickly took the boxes of tapes from my hands and rushed inside to cue up the first program to go on air. That program was in Italian.

We were thrilled to hear our theme song—"Lift Up the Trumpet, and Loud Let It Ring"—as the station identification was broadcast. The first voice was French: "*Ici* la Voix de l'Esperance"; next came German: "*Hier ist* die Stimme der Hoffnung." The last voice was mine in English: "This is *The Voice of Hope* on Adventist World Radio." For the first time, we were sending out a major challenge to the great countries of Europe that would not permit Adventist programs on local radio stations in their lands. But now we had a voice that would cover not only Europe but the Middle East and North Africa.

It was a high day, but I was exhausted. We made our way back into the city on the main highway that crossed the *Ponte Salazar*—the suspension bridge that spans the Tagus—into Lisbon's downtown. My only goal was to catch a couple of hours of sleep.

"Well, what happened—are we on the air?" James Aiken was on the line the next morning, anxiously wanting to know whether all had gone according to plan. I suddenly realized that in my excitement and exhaustion, I had forgotten to let the church headquarters in Washington know that the historic moment was a success.

"Yes, sir," I said. "Everything went according to plan, and Adventist World Radio is on the air." Now all we could do was wait for an answer to our constant prayers for a good response.

Five

The World Responds

Soon the letters began to arrive. As the office secretary, Andrea assumed the job of opening the mail that came in from around the world. She worked very hard to see that incoming mail was processed as soon as possible, and it grew into a full-time job. (Occasionally, Andrea would even let me help open the mail.) She organized a collection of promotional cards for Bible correspondence schools in all of our broadcast languages. She also composed letters answering any question a listener might have. These would go into an envelope with a special AWR card, called a QSL card. These cards were for listeners to report that they had heard our station.

Soon we learned that many regular shortwave listeners were also stamp collectors, so we purchased used stamps to slip into the envelopes as well. When we took the mail to the post office, we prayed that the recipients would respond by signing up for a Bible course.

"Listen to this," I excitedly told Andrea after I had opened one of the letters. "This man says he listens to us every evening from the tallest building in Europe—the towers of the Cologne Cathedral!" Employed as a watchman in the cathedral, he explained in his letter how each night, when he climbed one of the tall bell towers on his rounds, he took his portable shortwave receiver and listened to the world—a world that now included AWR!

His was our first letter from a DXer, that army of listeners who turned listening to distant radio stations into a hobby. These hobbyists became valuable allies in our work because they reported on the strength of our signal based on a numbered code. In return, we had a series of QSL cards—colorful postcard-sized replies—to send to verify the correctness of a DXer's report of our frequency's signal strength.

One person who became a valued long-distance friend was Arthur Cushen on the South Island of New Zealand. In spite of, or perhaps because of, his blindness, he was one of the world's most renowned international radio monitors. He was quick to let us know that he had received our broadcasts from Europe and, years later, the first to report hearing AWR's station on the island of Guam.

Heinz Haring, a DXer in Austria, also sent us a report shortly after he took up the hobby of DXing. He soon became a regular listener to AWR and requested a Bible study course, which he and his wife completed together. It wasn't long before his family was convicted of the truth of the Adventist message and became church members. It was the beginning of their longtime relationship with AWR. They began traveling to as many church facilities as possible, including our office in Lisbon, on their holiday vacations.

We soon realized the importance of the DX community in building a listenership: they tracked our broadcasts and then reported to their hobby clubs about AWR. With hundreds of clubs and thousands of members, these listeners formed an immediate audience for our programs and were active in telling others about them. I suggested to Andrea that we might do well to create our own DX program to attract this special set of listeners.

We found a list of clubs in a broadcast magazine and sent letters to each. "We'll give fifteen minutes once a week to the first one to respond to the letter," I said. The first to respond was Clive Jenkins, the president of the World DX Club in Britain. It was the start of a long relationship. He would write the script for the program, and we would record it for on air use. Eventually, AWR's Adrian Peterson began hosting our own DX program, which he called *Wavescan*. Later he renamed it *Radio Monitors International*, and it became one of the world's leading DX programs.

We received reception reports from all over Europe as well as other

The World Responds

parts of the world. Swedish radio aficionados were as keen as any nationality to hear radio stations far distant from their country. Since religious programs were not permitted on government-controlled Swedish radio, the only way private groups could broadcast to the country was to find airtime on stations outside the country.

Next door to our office on Rua Braamcamp was the office of IBRA Radio (International Broadcasting Radio Association) from the Pentecostal churches of Scandinavia. Eskil Johansson was the broadcast manager for that organization. It was he who first acted to obtain airtime on Radio Trans-Europe. *Perhaps AWR could direct programs to his homeland*, I thought, *just like he was doing.*

I decided to invite Gosta Wiklander, the communication director for the Swedish Union of Seventh-day Adventists, to come and visit us in Lisbon. He came and observed our operation and was impressed. He went back to his church administrators and convinced them to agree to begin Swedish programs on AWR.

Several years later, Gosta told me he was at a national radio conference in Sweden when he was introduced to the man in charge of the national radio network. The man asked him who he was and what his role was in radio. Gosta explained that because it was impossible to obtain airtime on the nation's radio networks, his programs were beamed into the country by shortwave from Portugal. "This is ridiculous," the man said. "Why should you not be on Swedish radio stations?" A couple of years later, the man was elected as a government leader and recalled his conversation with Gosta. He then led a campaign to permit religious organizations in Sweden to own and operate their own radio stations inside the country. Our church was quick to obtain radio licenses in two of Sweden's largest cities.

Another new program language that we were anxious to get on the air was Greek. When we arrived at Rua Braamcamp, we discovered that another new broadcaster on Radio Trans-Europe was an employee of the government of Greece, hired to read news of the home country to the Greek diaspora spread across Europe. Dr. Fernandez, the speaker, became a friend of the office staff. Often, we traveled together to the broadcast studio to deliver his and our programs.

Nick Germanis, a Greek immigrant to America, was eager to make a difference in his southern European home country. He called to ask whether there was any way he could sponsor a program on AWR. He was told, "Fortunately, there is a program by the Greek government on Radio Trans-Europe, and we can schedule a Greek program right after the Greek newscast—perfect!"

It turned out to be a good strategy but not in the way we expected. For five years, we were able to schedule our program to follow the Greek government's news program. Their program helped us to establish an audience of our own, with programs produced by Pastor Christoforides in Athens. And responses started coming in but mainly from central Europe: Germany, Austria, and Poland, where people had migrated for political reasons—to escape the politics of their home countries. People seemed thirsty for the messages in their own language and the hope that our programs gave them. They were exiles far from home and open to new revelations.

"Listen to this man's story," Andrea said one day. "He says he finally got the Bible we sent with tourists. He was so inspired by the Book we keep talking about on the radio that he began to search for one in Leipzig—the city where he lives." Her eyes danced with animation as she continued the story. "You remember, he's the man who asked for a Bible, but when we sent it, it was returned by the East German post office with 'address unknown'?" She continued, "Well, he wanted a copy of the Bible so much that he searched in bookstores in the city. Then he started asking at churches. He found an old Bible in one church, but it was in ancient Greek, which he couldn't read. Now he says he is a new man because of the Bible we sent." Later we found out the man became an Adventist and a member of our Adventist church in Leipzig.

Our members in Greece rejoiced to hear the many stories from these new church members—exiles across Europe. However, their disappointment was great at not hearing from any listeners in Greece itself, where we had only one church in the whole country. We keenly felt the disappointment ourselves, and when it came time to leave Portugal, we carried that disappointment with us.

Some years later, in 1989, we were told the most wonderful news. On our way to church meetings in Africa, our flight took us by way of Europe. We included a weekend in Athens on our itinerary to visit the ruins of the ancient city. On Sabbath, we set out early to find the Adventist church. We only knew the name of the street because we remembered hearing it so many times on the radio programs. We found

The World Responds

Keramikou Street and began walking down its sidewalk.

After two blocks, I noticed a man carrying a Bible under his arm, so I motioned to Andrea. She joined me as we followed the man who led us right to the church without knowing we were following. We received a typically warm welcome from the members there. When they found out we were from AWR, we were asked to give a report about the radio ministry. After church, an elderly gentleman pushed through the crowd to meet us.

"I'm Christoforides, the one who used to make programs for Portugal. Do you remember our contacts by telephone?" With a rush, the disappointment of all those years of no letters from Greece came back to me. "My wife and I invite you to our house for lunch. Can you come?"

We ate very well, enjoying the delicious Greek dishes that were set before us. After lunch, we talked about the church in Greece and the difficulties of growing an Adventist church in an Orthodox land. Then he had something special to tell us. "Do you remember our great disappointment because the radio programs got so little response from Greece?" he asked. "Well, we should have had more faith in the Lord. You know what happened?" By the twinkle in his eye, I knew he had exciting news.

"When the repressive government was thrown out, and democracy returned to our country, its native sons began to return. Some of them had become Seventh-day Adventists, thanks to AWR. They came back to their families in Macedonia, the northern province of Greece. They shared their new beliefs, and today we have three new churches where before we had none!" His eyes danced, and his cheeks creased. "All of a sudden, our membership doubled, and we had a new area of the country open to the gospel, with churches planted by God Himself."

We all had tears in our eyes as we realized what God had done.

Six

Secret Christians

Not long after our arrival in Portugal, we heard from our Paris studio crew about the fascinating way they were able to bring radio speakers together to record programs in Eastern European languages, such as Serbian, Croatian, Macedonian, and Slovenian. Once a year, they would have a summer recording session when speakers from Soviet Bloc countries would come, pretending to be on vacation, to the Adventist college in Croatia and spend long hours recording enough programs to fuel AWR for a year.

We decided to make the trip to Zagreb, Croatia, to witness this incredible event. We worked hard at the office to get our work prepared well ahead, then set out in our little blue Fiat 124. Our itinerary took us through the Extremadura region of eastern Portugal and western Spain, up along the French Riviera, then through Monaco and northern Italy to the Yugoslav border, where we would cross into the Soviet zone.

It was early evening when we arrived at Maruševec Castle outside Zagreb. The castle came into the church's hands when President Tito's government ordered the Seventh-day Adventists to move their seminary out of Belgrade. In return, the government allowed the church to establish its school in the old castle in northern Yugoslavia, provided the church would commit to restore and maintain the castle as a historic site.

Andrea and I were trying to follow a map in the dim evening light. We found the turns that were indicated but were surprised to find ourselves headed down a dirt road. We stopped to pore over the map and almost immediately found ourselves in the dust of a horse-drawn hay wagon that came upon us from behind.

"Maruševec, Maruševec," we shouted to two stout farm women walking beside the wagon. They replied with words in their own language and pointed in the direction we were headed. So we continued on.

"Welcome, welcome, please come in for supper," said the school principal when we finally arrived. The yogurt soup with solid brown bread tasted good. Hot tea and biscuits filled in the corners of our stomachs, which had not received solid food all day.

The most exciting part of our visit came the next day. We found that here, in the southern woods of Europe, nearly one hundred people had come to take part in the annual recording sessions. From sunup until late into the evening, the recording technicians from Paris kept at the work of recording speakers and music groups in five different languages. At the end of the two-week session, the technicians would pack up their makeshift studio and return to France with hundreds of tapes filled with material for the next season of programs on AWR.

"What a labor of love," exclaimed Andrea.

After the recording session, all those precious people returned to their home territories to listen to their programs on AWR and care for the requests from their listeners. This was the backbone of AWR's success. While Andrea and I were the only employees of AWR at the time, other church employees and volunteers from many countries were tasked with making sure we got the programs needed for on-air broadcasts. It was a successful cooperative strategy: AWR offered free airtime on its stations to local church territories while the local field supplied the programs that AWR broadcast back into the country of the program's origin.

Not only did this system prevent the need to establish and maintain large production centers at the broadcast station, but it also ensured that the programs were relevant and spoken by native speakers embedded in the life and trends of their society. It also made the whole process a family affair. All levels of the church were involved and cooperated with the Holy Spirit in the search for receptive minds hungering for words of hope.

The downside with this system was that the AWR staff found it rather difficult to obtain the thousands of personal stories of our listeners. That was the joy of workers in the local fields. Those of us keeping the programs going out through the airwaves were always eager to hear about the results of our efforts—the personal stories that bring so much satisfaction. It was also important to share these stories with our financial sponsors.

Our mail count kept climbing year by year. By our third year in Portugal, we counted nearly ten thousand pieces of mail processed. And sometimes our people on the ground in the local fields would share stories from their areas. The few that they shared fueled our enthusiasm.

One of the AWR speakers in Yugoslavia received a letter from a young man who had heard our program, had taken the Bible course, and requested that the speaker come to his town to baptize him as a new church member.

Consulting his schedule, the pastor wrote to the young man, telling him that it would be some weeks before he would be able to come to perform his baptism. When our speaker did arrive some weeks later, he found, to his surprise, the young man had twelve other people ready to be baptized with him! He had been busy sharing those Bible lessons with his friends.

One of the languages sponsored by our Paris studio was Arabic. In the first four years of broadcasts from Portugal, letters were received from Arabic-speaking listeners in twenty-seven countries! The Arabic Bible school averaged five hundred active students during those years. Pastor Pellicer, the founder of those broadcasts, kept very busy preparing radio programs, managing the Bible school, and personally visiting interested people in North Africa. He often shared very heartwarming stories with us.

"A young man wrote to the Bible school to say he was a longtime listener to AWR, and he wished to take the Bible course," he told us. "I could tell that he had an unusual sincerity about the subject, so I decided to send him the whole set of Life of Christ lessons. Within two weeks, all the completed lessons came back to us in the mail." Thus began an active correspondence between the listener and Pastor Pellicer. "A constant stream of questions indicated to us that he was delving deep into the Adventist message. We sent him the book *Steps to Christ* and a Bible."

The school was able to send him the address of an Adventist church. Shortly thereafter, the Bible school received the names and addresses of eight more young men whom this fellow had convinced to take the course. Needless to say, this young man soon became a Seventh-day Adventist, as did several of his friends.

"A young woman in Egypt fell into conversation with her Coptic Christian neighbors about Bible topics," Pastor Pellicer said as he started another story. "She had been given a Bible course enrollment card on the streets one day, and when she applied for the course, she was informed of the radio programs and started searching for the AWR signal." He told us that when her parents found out what she was doing, they threw her out of the house. "She remained true to her newfound faith, however, and was soon a church member."

Another young Muslim, a teenager who was known as the brightest lad in his class, heard our broadcasts and requested the Bible lessons. "He became so excited when the first lesson came that he decided to take it to school with him, hoping he would find time to work on the lesson there," Pastor Pellicer said. "He was so anxious to start filling out the lesson that during one class, every time the teacher turned to write on the blackboard, this lad opened his briefcase and tried to answer the Bible questions. But once he was not quick enough, and the professor saw him looking into his briefcase.

"The professor walked back to the student's desk, opened his briefcase, grabbed the Bible lesson, and said, 'You stay after class.' The boy was frightened, but after class, the professor looked over the lesson with him. The teacher became interested in the lesson, too, and asked whether the student would mind sharing the lesson study." Pastor Pellicer slapped his knee and concluded, "And that's how they both became our Bible course students."

Obviously, Pastor Pellicer was dedicated to his work and confident that the radio programs would bring many people in Arabic-speaking lands to Jesus. He turned serious. "Of course, people must be very careful. To become a Christian is very often the same as becoming a dead man," he said in a somber tone. "It is contrary to the Muslim culture, so most Christians there must become secret believers."

In 1975, one of the highlights at the Adventist seminary in Collonges-sous-Salève, France, was the emotional baptism of a young Arabic-speaking man whose first contact with Seventh-day Adventism was through AWR and the Arabic Bible course. In giving his personal testimony, this handsome youth told of his search early in life for something fulfilling.

"My parents were able to steer me clear of many obstacles, such as drinking and smoking," he said in his testimony. "But when I was twenty, some friends of mine tricked me into taking some drugs with a soft drink. This led me into the drug scene." He became very quiet and took a deep breath. "Some months later, I realized what a terrible path I was following. I regretted these steps, and one day I decided that I would go back to my old hobby of stamp collecting to occupy my time.

"A friend told me that the Voice of Prophecy Bible School sent stamps to anyone requesting them, so I wrote to the Bible school and asked for stamps and, at the same time, signed up for the course they offered. This led me to a new spiritual experience, and I decided I would go to the Adventist college in France." While there, he was welcomed into the Seventh-day Adventist Church as a member.

A story similar to this was repeated some years later. A young man listened to our programs over a period of several months and became convinced that the Lord was calling him to Christianity. He could find no Adventist church in his city in North Africa, but he did find a small evangelical group that he joined clandestinely.

He wanted to be baptized as an Adventist but decided to accept baptism by the evangelical group, saying in his heart that he was really being baptized as a Seventh-day Adventist. About that time, he fell in love with a lovely young woman and immediately faced the dilemma of figuring out how he could tell her that he had become a Christian.

He began by telling her about one Christian belief that he thought a woman would like to hear: Christian men marry only one wife, marriage for Christians is a lifelong commitment, and women are considered equal to men in the Christian home. Before long, he had her convinced that Christianity was the right religion—and that she ought to marry him! After that, he went to study theology at the Adventist college in France, where he completed his course as a religion major.

Church leaders heard about him and invited him to become a radio speaker for *The Voice of Hope*. Andrea and I asked him how he planned to attract his people to the Christian message. "I will tell them about

Secret Christians

God's love," he said confidently, "because it is something they don't know about or understand." He went on to become a radio pastor to thousands of secret Christians in Arabic-speaking lands.

It is just such stories that make us long for the day when we will meet face-to-face with those thousands of people who are obliged to follow their convictions secretly and suffer the loneliness of being outcasts in their own families and societies.

Seven

Life in Portugal

"Here, kitty, kitty. Here, kitty, kitty." Andrea can never resist a quick friendship with any cat that is within view, and this one, a Siamese with a crooked tail, was especially fetching. "Here, kitty, kitty," she tried again, but she was too late. The cat had slipped through an ornate gate that opened onto a drive where a black Toyota sedan was parked.

We had returned from Croatia and were back in Portugal, taking one of our occasional walks through the Belém neighborhood near our apartment building. The sloping hillside was bathed in the afternoon sun. We were planning to continue to the top of the slope to visit a model windmill located there. We saw many windmills like this in the countryside far from the city, but this one was in the middle of a small city park, obviously put there for tourists, so they wouldn't have to drive far to see an authentic Portuguese windmill.

When we signed the rental agreement for our little fourth-floor apartment, we didn't realize the neighborhood was actually known as the diplomatic part of Lisbon. But as we walked the area, we soon noticed some of the large homes nearby were ambassadorial residences. A couple of them also served as embassies of smaller countries, while the major European countries and the larger countries from the Americas, Asia, and Africa had big embassies downtown.

Life in Portugal

As we stood in front of the driveway, looking beyond the gate and trying to see where the friendly cat had gone, we suddenly heard a voice. "Well, hello, how do you do?" We looked up to see a white-haired gentleman dressed in a black suit.

"We were just admiring your little cat," Andrea offered as an excuse for lingering at his front gate.

"Are you French, Swedish, British?" he asked in English.

"Well, we're American, and we were just out for a walk and were enticed by your little cat," I said.

"Please come in for a visit. I am absolutely alone, absolutely alone. Do you have time to come in for tea?" he blurted out the gracious invitation.

That was the beginning of our long friendship with Senhor João de Melo—a retired military officer, the nephew of a former prime minister, an elder in the noble Melo family, a father of three, and a widower now for four years. He became our tutor on Portuguese life, our talking historian, our teacher in Old World culture, and most of all, our dear, dear friend. This visit was the first of many.

Upon entering his house, we realized his loneliness was due to being widowed, for his home certainly was not without occupants. We were introduced to his cook, his gardener, and his secretary-chauffeur. But socially, he was alone, and he, therefore, seemed delighted to make our acquaintance. We became his audience as he took us on a tour of his extensive garden while he told us his life stories when he had reveled with the royal princes and princesses of Portugal. He shared his old photo albums and delighted us with traditional Portuguese foods. His cook's chocolate mousse was legendary.

Even though he repeated himself over and over, it was a pleasure to hear him recall the stories, which will never be erased from our memories, that gave us pictures of Portuguese life. We gained a special insight into how life operated in this incredible country and its past greatness and nobility.

We soon learned that "come to tea," in Senhor João's vocabulary, was somewhat like the British idea of high tea we had heard about. Biscuits with spreads, bread, sweets, and other small edibles were all part of "tea." Taking tea was often expanded to a full-course meal at Senhor João's.

"You must come to visit me in my summer home at Sintra," he

suggested one day in late spring. "It becomes so stifling hot here in the city that we are forced to go up to the mountains to escape the heat." He explained that this was a traditional annual migration, going back to royal times when the king and leading families would seek higher ground to avoid the sweltering Lisbon summers.

The Sintra Mountains, less than an hour's drive from downtown Lisbon, were, indeed, Lisbon's paradise retreat. Several old castles adorned the mountaintops. Large manor homes, public promenades, and lush gardens surrounded the center of Sintra. As an added divine touch, at the foot of the mountains on the side opposite Lisbon, white sandy beaches on the shore of the Atlantic Ocean glistened like diamonds from our viewpoint in the town of Sintra. While the oldsters relaxed in the cool shade at the mountaintops, their grandchildren and great-grandchildren headed for the beach.

Upon our arrival, we rang the bell at the estate entrance and waited as a maid in a white dress opened the creaking ivy-covered gate. She pointed to a house half hidden from view by flowering shrubs and oak trees. We drove down the winding gravel drive and stopped before an impressive ancient gray house. Our eyes fell upon the central point of the scene—an ornate gurgling fountain in the middle of a large gravel parking area.

"Welcome, welcome; I was afraid you would not find me," Senhor João greeted us as we climbed out of our car. In his usual fashion, we first had to be given a tour of the estate. He walked us back up the drive to the house of his sister, the Countess of Cartaxo. A slim female version of Senhor João, she was most gracious and witty. They talked of the old days when they were young and their families spent the summer months in Sintra. Upon the death of their parents, she inherited the main house, and João got the stables, which he promptly turned into a magnificent family vacation home of his own.

"Come, I've arranged dinner for just the three of us," he announced. "All the grandchildren have gone to the beach, and my son and daughter are still at work in the city, so we are very much alone."

As we entered the dining room, we gasped at the sight of the long linen-covered table stretched before us. The table was long enough to seat two dozen people in this ornate banquet hall, which previously housed the horse stables. The three of us, however, were seated at one end of the table and enjoyed another conversation about the weather;

the old days in Sintra, when this table was fully surrounded by loved ones; and the latest news about his family. We had come to know most of his immediate family, so we were able to make sincere inquiries about his son, the banker; his son-in-law, the professor; or their sons and daughters, who were university students at the time.

To say that our friendship with Senhor João was a treat would be an understatement. For us, he represented Portugal in its fullness. For him, we were his surprise friends during his old age. He depended on us to make life meaningful at a time when he needed friends the most, and his world was changing at a confusing rate.

When we left Portugal, after our five years there, we continued our friendship by letter until one day an envelope arrived, written by an unfamiliar hand. It was from his daughter, informing us of his passing in 1979 at nearly ninety years of age. She thanked us for our friendship, which she said had meant so much to her father in recent years. For our part, Andrea and I could both say, "Senhor João, the pleasure was all ours."

Forever after, in our minds, Senhor João epitomized the loving people of Portugal. We found that this same love and concern were shown at all levels of society. The graciousness we found in him, we also found in the hundreds of dear church members who became friends for life. The hospitality we found in his home, we also found in all Portuguese homes to which we were frequently invited. The steadfast friendship he showered upon us was the very same shown to us by numerous people we came to know and love.

But when we first arrived in Lisbon, we were strangers, and we did not speak Portuguese. Language classes quickly brought us up to speed, thanks to our previous exposure and college classes in Spanish and French.

During our first winter, we spent many Saturday nights alone in our apartment, snuggled around the little propane space heater, reading books from Andrea's cache and other books that we could check out from the library that the United States Information Services maintained in the city.

One of the first important activities for any Adventist moving to a new location is to find a church home. We started visiting the churches in Lisbon one by one. Our hearts were captured by one church in the suburbs that was full of young people and led by a dynamic pastoral duo—Pastor Pires and his wife, Maria Augusta—who welcomed us with open arms.

The young people of the Amadora Seventh-day Adventist Church bombarded us with questions in their halting English: "Does it snow in America?" "Do you know any American Indians?" "How big is New York?" We couldn't help but love these vivacious young people. Soon we were inviting them to our place for cookies and Bible studies on Friday nights, hiking with them on Saturday afternoons, and socializing with them on Saturday nights. I was asked to be the youth counselor, and we both joined the choir and became totally immersed in church life.

Two years after we arrived, Pastor Pires was hospitalized for an illness; his symptoms were compounded by injuries he had suffered in an automobile accident some years before. His health situation deteriorated, and within weeks, he passed away. We joined in the sorrow of our church family. One of the most profound moments in my life came when we, as a corporate church family, were proceeding to the cemetery where we would lay our good pastor until resurrection morning.

Andrea and I plodded down the road, following the coffin held aloft by young men from the church. I felt an arm take mine. One of the young men was pulling me forward so that I could take a pallbearer position. With a heavy heart, I bore the burden of the coffin with five others. From then on, I had no doubt that I was a member of that church family. How could one become more integrated than to be invited to share in so intimate a duty?

Sometime later, I was trying to explain our decision to change churches after three years at Amadora. "We feel the Lord has a special work for us to do in the city." The members were having difficulty in accepting that we were actually going to leave their membership.

"Brother Steele is right," I heard the approving voice of Maria Augusta, who was now, after the death of her husband, pastoring the church.

"He's right. We here at Amadora have active young people, a full church with standing-room only, and a great church family. The Central Lisbon church has young people but no leaders. Their pews are full of old people, and they need help. Even though we will miss our beloved sister and brother, we must do this to help the church revive its youth activities." Her words were accepted as final.

Our first priority at the Central Lisbon Seventh-day Adventist

Life in Portugal

Church was to start a Junior Sabbath School class for Bible study. We were able to convert a downstairs classroom for our use, and soon it was packed every week. The children thrived, knowing we had a special program for them.

These juniors were in the Pathfinder Club age range, and having been a Pathfinder myself back in my home church in Florida, I had a huge appreciation for the character-building nature of the Pathfinder program developed by the church. Like the Boy Scouts, it involved practical skills in camping and arts and crafts. I knew it would be a huge task with risks of all kinds. But these city children desperately needed to gain the confidence that comes from learning extra skills outside their school classroom. For my part, I was stepping into an environment where confidence can be built, but actions are sometimes easily misunderstood—a reality that all youth leaders must balance.

We invited children from Adventist families and from the chuch neighborhood to be part of Portugal's first Pathfinder Club. Within a year, five of the children responded to our invitation to become church members. One, Maria de Rosario Raposo, became like our own daughter, and when we returned to the United States, she came to live in our home while studying at Andrews University.

There's always at least one challenging lad in any organization, and one Pathfinder boy became my own special challenge because he was always talking out of turn and goading the other boys into foolishness. Often on camping trips, he would bring me to my wit's end. On one occasion, I sent him to sit in a tree, like a chirping bird, because he couldn't keep his mouth closed for two minutes! Twelve years later, when we returned to Lisbon for a visit, he insisted on talking to me when he saw me at church. He wanted me to know that his Pathfinder experience changed his life—he was now teaching high school physical education! Such are the rewards when working with young people.

A dozen years later, a Portuguese pastor informed me that Portugal now had more Pathfinder Clubs than any other country in Europe, thanks to that first club we started.

"Brother Steele, will you lead out in our first Junior youth camp?" the church's youth director for Portugal asked a few months before we left Portugal. At the time, I was desperately trying to wrap up my AWR work so I could reach Andrews University in time for the start of classes. After five years of being asked whether we could "stay one more year," I made the decision that it was time to return to the United States for more schooling.

"Well, I can't possibly lead out in the camp, but I am willing to attend and help out," I replied cautiously.

It was glorious late summer, and we drove for four hours to reach the church youth camp at Figueira da Foz. The open-air gym-cafeteria was located several hundred feet back from the Atlantic Ocean's beach. Tents were to be our home for the week. I arrived just before the scheduled staff meeting was to begin.

"We are assembled here for the first Junior youth camp in the history of the church in Portugal," said the youth leader to the assembled staff. "And I would like to present to you the director of our camp, Allen Steele." I was in shock! Nothing further had been said since our brief chat the week before. I never agreed to be camp leader, but it would be embarrassing to reject the job after such an introduction. Fortunately, we had a very good group of camp counselors. *Here I am; I'll have to make it work*, I thought.

The days were filled with camp crafts, swims at the beach, and games. At night, we showed nature films borrowed from embassy libraries in Lisbon. As the weekend neared, my thoughts turned to Fernando. He was a conscientious young man in his early twenties who had been coming to our Pathfinder meetings with his little sister. Her parents would not allow her to come to the meetings by herself, so Uncle Fernando was recruited to be her chaperone.

He was interested in our club activities and always was there to help in any way he could, so I asked him to be a counselor. We had Bible studies together, and I felt his heart was open to God's leading. "Fernando," I said on one of the last evenings of the camp, "you have been with us for over a year. You obviously agree with everything we teach, and you've been faithful at all our meetings. How would you like to be baptized here at camp this weekend as an example to these young people?"

"I think I would like that," he said in his nonchalant way. His baptism was the climax of the camp, and many of the children in the final assembly raised their hands when asked if they would like to prepare to do the same thing.

Eight

Can You Stay Another Year?

"I can see it now," I yelled to Andrea above the traffic noise. "It's a Pan Am 747. See that little white dot in the western sky?"

We were at Lisbon's Portela Airport, awaiting the arrival of Walter Scragg, our first visitor from the church's world headquarters in Washington, DC. Shortly after we moved to Lisbon, Walter was appointed as director of the Radio and Television Department when James Aitken became the church's ambassador to the United Nations.

Our most recent correspondence from Walter was not encouraging. He said that AWR's financial situation was concerning and that we might not be able to continue our AWR work from Portugal. He would be coming to pay us a visit. We had been praying for days, ever since he told us, and we were somewhat anxious about further news he might bring.

"I have good news for you," he said as we piled into our Volkswagen Microbus for the trip to the office. "Things have turned around. After I told you we were low on funds for AWR, we worked on a little report for the back page of the *Review* [the official church magazine for members]. We mentioned the challenge we have to keep the radio programs going, and within two months, enough funds came in to cover next year!" He gave us his big smile and added, "Isn't God good?"

We sighed in relief. We couldn't bear the thought of cutting our work short. Our program producers were doing well at keeping the programs coming to us. New studios in Sweden, England, and the Netherlands were going into production. AWR's existence was threatened just when we were in expansion mode. And listeners were responding. We had received one thousand letters in the first few months on the air.

We could tell Walter was relieved too. What had happened with the *Review*'s article became a pattern for continuing during the first few years of AWR. When we faced a shortfall of funds, Walter would crank up his writing arm with news that we sent him and print an article in the church paper, and miraculously, church members would respond, and AWR would receive another extension of life.

"I've been authorized to ask if you two are willing to stay another year in Portugal," he said when we arrived at the office.

"Of course, we are," we both chimed in. "We feel we've only begun."

It was great fun to have a visitor. Not many church leaders came to Lisbon since it is not really on the way to most of Europe's other major cities. But when they did come, it was a great boost to our morale. It was also exciting for those who came to see AWR in action, and the Radio Trans-Europe staff were always happy to show off the station's facilities.

The on-air studio in Sesimbra and the transmitter site in Sines were required visits for anyone coming to see AWR in action. Both of these facilities were operated and maintained by Deutsche Welle (German Wave), which is Germany's international broadcast organization. Radio Trans-Europe's one transmitter was owned by the Trémoulet family, but Deutsche Welle had two transmitters in the station, serving as a relay for transmissions from their main studios in Cologne. As years passed and AWR's need for more airtime increased, a second transmitter carried some of the Adventist programs.

The trip to Sesimbra was a picturesque drive. The first segment was the Salazar Bridge over the wide estuary of the Tagus River. (It reminded me of the Golden Gate Bridge in San Francisco, California.) When it was built, the bridge was named after the country's ruling dictator, then later renamed the 25 de Abril Bridge (April 25) when democracy was declared in 1974.

Once across the bridge on the south side of the river, there was a stretch of about nine miles (fifteen kilometers) of Portugal's only

Can You Stay Another Year?

express highway at the time (save for a short stretch north of the city). Upon leaving the expressway, the remaining journey was across Cabo Espichel—a high cape dotted with small farms and herds of sheep. This last section of the trip was the most pleasant. I was always thankful for my weekly trip to Sesimbra to deliver programs when I passed through this lovely countryside.

On one occasion, I stopped near a little stone barn, just to see what it contained and study how it was built. When I walked around the corner of the little whitewashed building, I gazed upon a most tranquil scene. A big white sow lay on her side, snoring in the warm afternoon sun with a dozen little pink piglets stretched out, sound asleep, between her legs. I quietly took my camera from my shoulder bag to record this peaceful scene.

The click of the shutter awakened a little black-and-white kitten nearby, which I had not even noticed. Upon waking, the little tiger began hissing and spitting with a great show. Her display awakened a couple of the piglets, and instantly, pandemonium broke loose. Squealing pigs and startled cats started jumping in all directions. I made a hasty retreat, happy that I'd been able to capture that pastoral scene before the mayhem ensued.

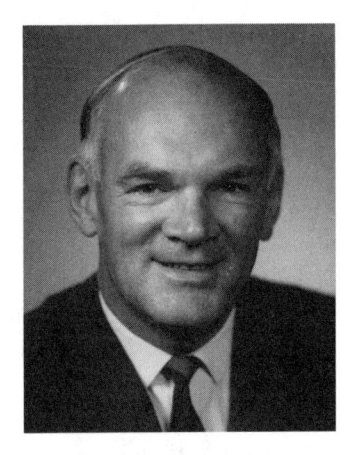

Walter Scragg of the Radio and Television Department at church world headquarters was instrumental in getting AWR on the air and later was AWR's first president, from 1991 to 1995.

A narrow, winding road descends precipitously from the cape to the white sand beach where the little fishing village of Sesimbra lies. In summer, it is a lively holiday resort, but for most of the year, it is somnolent—except when the fishing boats come in. On those occasions, the whole beach awakens into a giant fish market.

The Radio Trans-Europe on-air studio was built near this picturesque town so that it could have a direct line of sight for microwave links with the transmitter site in Sines, which is around thirty miles (fifty kilometers) farther south on the same coast. The trip south to Sines is through one of Portugal's largest cork forests. It is a remarkable experience to see these trees, which are members of the oak genus. Their trunks, stripped of the bark, reveal a range of gold, orange, and brown colors, depending on how recently the bark was stripped.

During the time we lived in Portugal, the town of Sines—the birthplace of Vasco da Gama, the great Portuguese explorer—was also a sleepy fishing village. The small man-made harbor accommodated only a dozen colorful fishing boats, which bobbed in the tidal waters of the shore. On days when there was no ocean breeze, the air was stifling hot. At midday, the whole town came to a standstill for siesta.

A few miles outside of town is a large hill named *Monte Mudo* (Silent Mountain). This spot near the Atlantic shore, where the transmitters of Radio Trans-Europe were located, was calculated to be the best location in Europe for optimal propagation of shortwave signals to Europe, North Africa, and the Middle East. The transmitter building, backed up by a number of antennas, was a modern building of utilitarian design. Inside, the air conditioning helped to keep the transmitters and the engineers cool because the huge 250-kilowatt transmitters put out a lot of heat when transmitting.

The silence in the antenna field at this remote place always overwhelmed me. Only two distinct sounds come to mind as I remember standing among the antennas. The gentlest winds caused a rushing sound when they passed through the antennas, stretched up against the sky. When I heard that sound, I prayed that the winds would carry God's message swiftly across the mountains and valleys to homes where eager ears waited to hear. The other sound that floated in the air came from the surrounding farms where braying burros and donkeys provided animal power for farm work and transportation to town for their owners.

Our office in Lisbon and these two facilities at Sesimbra and Sines combined to provide a powerful voice to reach a potential audience of over five hundred million people in the three target zones of the station. It was always a thrill to bring visitors to these incredible facilities where they could witness firsthand what God had provided.

The electricity grid south of Lisbon was unreliable, so occasionally, our broadcasts were not aired. Thus, we had a bone to pick with the station ownership, headed by Guy Comminges. He visited us at the

Can You Stay Another Year?

Rua Braamcamp office one summer, and the loss of airtime was the main topic of our discussion. He assured us it was "an act of God" that could not be helped. As the manager of Radio Antilles on the island of Montserrat in the Caribbean, Comminges became friends with the Adventist governor's family, and he thus felt a close connection to AWR.

A few months after Walter Scragg's visit, we were delighted to welcome an incredible couple—Willma and Olov Blomquist. Dr. Blomquist had a Scandinavian background, so he and his wife had a special interest in seeing Scandinavian countries included in AWR's reach. They shed tears of joy when they saw what God was doing through AWR. Their enthusiasm was enormous, and their friendship soon developed into a mentorship of other young AWR employees, including us.

Back in the office after our tour of the station's facilities, we were happy to tell the Blomquists the latest stories from listeners around Europe. Andrea had been in touch with a young lady in Sweden who lived near the Norwegian border. "She says she had never heard of Seventh-day Adventists before she heard our broadcast, and when she finished our Bible correspondence course, she didn't know how to find an Adventist church. Finally, a pastor from a church two hundred kilometers [124 miles] away was able to come by train to visit her. He baptized her, and now once a month, she travels by train to church."

"And what about this man in Germany?" I suggested. "He listened to our program, signed up for the Bible course, and decided to become a Christian. But which church? While he was studying our Bible course, another Christian man had been visiting him weekly to study the Bible. Feeling it was time to decide, he prayed and asked God to send an Adventist to his door the next day if that was the path he was to follow.

"The next day an Adventist pastor who had been alerted to the man's situation by AWR went to visit him. He accepted it as the sign he asked of God. But there's more to the story," I added. "He is partially blind and now helps translate Christian literature into Braille for our Bible school in Darmstadt."

Another man in Germany who worked as a forest ranger had a habit of carrying a small shortwave radio on his shoulder. One day he suddenly heard a station he had never heard before—AWR. Listening became a habit, and soon he signed up for the Bible course and later became an Adventist.

"Wait till you hear this one," Andrea said. "A family in the Swiss Alps started listening to our programs and decided they wanted to become Christians. Only one problem: the family owned a tavern, and they knew they couldn't, in good conscience, continue their business." But the high point of the story was yet to come.

"Their little six-year-old girl came up with a terrific idea," Andrea explained. " 'Let's turn our tavern into a milk bar,' she suggested. 'We can sell milk, cheese, ice cream, and yogurt.' Well, that's what they did," Andrea continued, "and they report business is booming."

"There's a family of six who were recently baptized as a result of listening to AWR." I thought Willma and Olov would enjoy this story because the family had sent us a picture of themselves on their baptismal day. "They are Ukrainians who were able to immigrate to France. Being far from home, they listened to the radio to see whether they could find a Ukrainian station. What they found was the Ukrainian *Voice of Hope* on AWR. They embraced the message and enrolled in the Bible course."

Shortly after the Blomquists visited us, we were delighted to hear that he was appointed as a member of the newly established AWR board of directors. Subsequently, whenever we were at the board meetings, we always reserved time to be with the Blomquists for an AWR "storyathon."

Nine

Challenging the Giant

Our experience at the big recording session in Croatia was the highlight of our first years with AWR. Not too long afterward, we agreed to spend a few days of vacation in the Iron Curtain countries with some dear Portuguese friends. This trip took us into Czechoslovakia and Hungary. The trip gave us a firsthand view of what life was like for people under Communist rule.

In Prague, we listened as our tour guide derided the Russian soldiers we saw around town who were sent to "protect" the Czechoslovakian citizens. We felt bad for the family in Budapest who moved out of their house to sleep in tents in the backyard so they could rent their house to us for one night to gain some desperately needed extra income. We were also distressed when the lady of the house asked us for used clothing, and we had nothing to give her because we were traveling with only enough clothes to make it through the trip.

We were intrigued by the black market money changers in Bratislava. At the hotel where we stayed, the cashier had two money drawers—one that would record transactions for government scrutiny and the other for black market exchanges.

We met with challenges in finding food that was recognizable to us. One of our best finds was an outdoor restaurant where the one

God's Air Force

item on the menu was Hungarian goulash. The menu said the goulash came with a side salad; it turned out to be a large slice of dill pickle. Upon our departure from the Soviet sector, we entered Austria and immediately began our search for another restaurant.

It was late evening when we saw a restaurant sign in the dim light in the first town across the border. We entered and asked for a menu. Our meal included a steaming bowl of noodle soup, fresh bread, huge three-egg omelets for each of us, and a fresh green salad—a real salad. It seemed like a banquet. We couldn't stop laughing as we each complained that our shrunken stomachs didn't seem able to hold all that incredible food. That meal was the topic of conversation all the way back home.

AWR on Radio Trans-Europe was only one station that was aiming programs at the Soviet Union; other Western countries were also flooding the airwaves over Russia. Our Russian and Ukrainian programs were produced by the *Voice of Prophecy* in California. Because mail service between the West and Soviet Bloc states was virtually nonexistent or highly censored, we could only guess what effect our broadcasts to that part of the world were having.

We knew our programs were having at least some results from the simple fact that Radio Moscow was constantly jamming our transmitter's frequencies. We also knew that the Soviets had huge fields of transmitters that they could use to jam our frequency either by airing Radio Moscow on that same frequency or by using noise machines to make our frequency unlistenable. In order to stay ahead of their jamming tactics, our frequencies were often changed by Radio Trans-Europe's engineers. Our best source of information about what was happening in Russia was from tourists who were able to get visas to enter Eastern Europe and would report what they heard and saw in that area when they returned to the West.

We heard one incredible story because of its Western connection. A member of the Communist Party in Russia started listening to AWR and decided he wanted to take the free Bible course that was offered. He knew he didn't dare receive the lessons through the mail at his office or home address. So he began to think about how he might receive the lessons without anyone at home knowing it.

It so happened that his diplomatic job required travel to the Russian embassy in Rome three times a year, and he thought maybe he could have the lessons sent to himself somewhere in Italy. He decided to ask his Italian barber whether the lessons could be mailed to the barber and saved for his regular visit. His plan was successful because we know he completed all the lessons; however, we never learned the final outcome of his experience. We guessed his tactic was discovered, and he might have been transferred to a new assignment that kept him in Russia.

There are many stories about AWR's attempts to reach the world for Jesus that did not reveal immediate results. Our constant challenge to break through the Iron Curtain turned out to be one of the most spectacular. When Communism fell in Russia, new doors opened in that great country, which we could never have imagined in the early days of AWR.

In 1988, Andrea and I, along with another Adventist couple, decided that it would be a great experience to take the Trans-Siberian Railway across seven of the eleven Russian time zones, from Irkutsk in Siberia to Moscow, and then on to the Baltic Sea at St. Petersburg. We had vacation time on our hands, so we determined to fly to Beijing and take the train from there to Irkutsk and hop on the Trans-Siberian to cross the vast steppes and forests of that great country to Moscow, then to St. Petersburg.

In Beijing, we took time to visit the city center and the Great Wall of China. Then it was time to board the Chinese train that would take us north through Mongolia to the Russian border and Irkutsk, the main city in Siberia. We'll never forget traveling through the night in the dusty desert of Inner Mongolia and then into the flatlands of the country of Mongolia itself. In the early morning, we arrived at Mongolia's capital and foremost city, Ulaanbaatar. There the train stopped for a little over an hour, and we had the opportunity to enjoy the view from the railroad station overlooking the city.

We then boarded the train for another night ride across the darkened landscape of northern Mongolia to the Russian border, around the southern end of Lake Baikal, and into the city of Irkutsk, arriving very early on a Sunday morning while the city was still asleep. We had most of the day to explore this fabled city, but knowing nothing about the place and because there was no activity at that time of the morning, we just started walking through the streets and came to a lovely green city park. We sat down on a bench to wait for the city to wake up.

Soon an elderly man came staggering along the pathway, obviously a bit tipsy from too much vodka. When he saw us, he stopped to chat, not realizing that we were foreigners. In our own broken way, we attempted to tell him we were American tourists. After we repeated ourselves several times, he finally caught on to what we were saying. As soon as it dawned on him that we were Americans, he started to run through the park, yelling what we concluded was "The Americans are here; the Americans are here!" at the top of his voice.

Eventually, the city came alive, and we went walking downtown. The famous ancient houses of Irkutsk were charming. Many were made of weathered wood that had lost any paint that they might have had. But the doors and windowpanes were painted in bright colors with window boxes for flowers. Some had cats sleeping in the closed windows, enjoying the morning rays of sunshine.

At midday, we started looking for a place to eat. Searching for food became a daily mission in Russia. On this day, we entered a place that looked like a food kitchen. From the order counter, we could look into the kitchen area, where we saw large trays of what we discovered to be sheep brains lined in rows. Now that's a meal that is not appetizing to vegetarians! So we settled for a bowl of noodle soup and hard bread.

Fortunately, we had brought a couple of suitcases full of snacks and instant soups, so we knew we would have more food when we got back to the train. A real blessing on the train was the hot water samovar in each car for making hot tea. We had also purchased a large bag of apples in China, and those turned out to be a prized possession. In Irkutsk, we also found a grocery store that had mostly empty shelves, except for bottles and bottles of home-canned fruit. We noticed people crowded around a large container on the floor, so we joined them to see what all the excitement was about. There was the main fresh food item of the day—a barrel of cucumbers. We felt fortunate that we could afford to buy some.

That afternoon we stepped into a Russian Orthodox Church to observe a priest swinging incense pots from sacred spot to sacred spot around the church. A small crowd of believers followed his steps and reverently listened to his incantations. At one point, I found myself standing next to a young man who was watching intently. I asked him if he spoke English, and to my surprise, he answered yes. I asked if he had a Bible, and he answered no. I told him what time our train was leaving, and if he could meet us there, I would give him a Bible. He was very excited at the thought of having his own Bible.

He showed up at the train station, and I happily gave him the Bible. He thanked me over and over. He waved goodbye as the train pulled away.

Our train was quite late in departing, which was the story of the rest of our trip across the country—late arrivals and late departures. Often it would be several hours late, even though it was called the Siberian Express. For nearly five days, we crossed the endless expanses of the Russian terrain. We experienced the wideness of the steppes, the open prairies, and the Ural Mountains. The train occasionally made short stops at various cities. At one stop, we were pleased to find some babushkas selling tin buckets of boiled potatoes. They were the best things we had eaten in days.

One day we decided to try lunch in the dining car. As we neared the dining room, we passed a door to the kitchen and looked in. We saw a hog carcass hanging from a high hook. Flies were swarming all over the meat, and the sight and smell turned our stomachs, so we retreated to our cabin and looked for something more appetizing in our food suitcase.

Finally, we came to Moscow. We were whisked to the hotel where we thought we had reservations, only to find there were no rooms available, even though our trip was fully arranged by the state-run Intourist travel agency. We checked on another hotel nearby, but it was also full. Back at our assigned hotel, dozens of people were sprawled on the lobby sofas with their luggage. It was looking like we would spend the night in the lobby, but then one of the ladies at the check-in counter motioned for me to come close. Speaking German, she said she had one small room with two single beds that she could let us have. We accepted without question. At least we had a place to sleep on two single beds and makeshift mats on the bare floor.

The next day we set out again on our perennial search for food. Lines of people stretched for blocks, and we knew they must be purchasing food or other household commodities, but we didn't know what. Andrea decided she would wait in line, no matter how long it took, to get to the little shop that was selling some kind of food. The reward for her perseverance was a couple of tomatoes.

Then we were off to St. Petersburg—the most incredible part of our trip. This was the northernmost point of our travels. We arrived on a

Friday in midsummer, and sunset wasn't until after 9 p.m., which gave us time to take in a circus performance while it was yet light. The next day, being Sabbath, we determined to find an Adventist church. We were successful as well as delighted to meet with a full church of about a hundred people. There was excitement in the air, and the buzz of whispers made us curious to find out what was happening. We were told there was to be a baptism—the first in seventy years! We witnessed the ceremony and joy of the congregation as five people professed their faith in Jesus through immersion in a baptismal pool, which was revealed by the removal of floorboards in the middle of the sanctuary. We also heartily congratulated the new church members.

One of them, a medical doctor, spoke English and indicated he would enjoy visiting with us later and invited us to his home that evening. His lovely wife worked in a bakery and was able to offer us slices of chocolate cake along with tea. Also in the group were several of their friends; one was an architect who answered our questions about the beautiful, ornate buildings in the city. He told us that the city required the facades to be maintained impeccably, but inside many of the buildings were ramshackle.

The group was anxious to learn about life in America, and we asked many questions about life in Russia. The conversation was robust and delightful. The doctor commented on the chocolate cake we were eating. He said he couldn't afford to purchase such a thing, but he was proud that his wife had more privileges than he and that she was able to obtain it from her bakery. We also learned they were on the list for a new refrigerator and a car—both of which they thought they might obtain within a couple of years. They also hoped one day to have a home of their own. In their present dwelling, they had to share the kitchen and bathroom with occupants in the apartment next door.

To our surprise, they wanted to talk about Alaska. They maintained that one of the great regrets of the Russian people was their country's sale of that territory to the United States. They showed us a big hardbound picture book about Russian Alaska. It obviously was an important topic to them, whereas to most Americans, that far northern state is a distant and unknown land.

We talked late into the night. Our train would take us to Helsinki in the morning, so we finally, regretfully, had to say goodbye to those precious people. But their loveliness was foremost in our minds ever after. When we got back home, we sent them a package of a few basic food items and other delicacies, but we never heard another word from them. We worried that the package was confiscated. We also wrote a letter of thanks for their hospitality but received no reply.

Our exposure to Communist Russia was an important education. How we longed for the day when communication with our people there would open opportunities for advancing God's cause. And then it happened!

In 1989, the year after our visit, Communism fell, and doors were opened for tremendously advancing God's mission to the largest country in the world.

Kenneth Mittleider, the new AWR board vice chair, and Walter Scragg, the AWR director, traveled to Siberia to negotiate terms to rent airtime on Radio Moscow transmitters that were sitting idle at a huge antenna farm. A number of these transmitters were the very ones that previously were used to block AWR programs from Portugal! AWR was the first religious organization to broadcast across the vast region from those very 250-kilowatt transmitters! The broadcasts began on March 1, 1992.

Walter said it was -40 degrees Celsius (also -40 degrees Fahrenheit) in Novosibirsk when they met with the operators of the Siberian stations. While there, he heard the story of a church member who lived in the area. This man had a great desire: every time he walked near those Radio Moscow transmitters, he prayed that one day they would be made to work for the Lord. He lived to see his dream come true.

When democracy was declared, the Seventh-day Adventist Church quickly went into action to evangelize the country. Ours was the first church to build and begin operating a publishing house for printing Christian literature in the Russian language. The church also started a college in a city some distance south of Moscow. And a media center was built in the city of Tula to create radio and television programs. It was my privilege to serve as a consultant for this ministry that was led by young Peter Kulakov, who became a dear friend and collaborator in Adventist media ministry. I was also able to join him for an evangelistic campaign in the city of Kazan, Russia. Under his leadership, our church soon had a radio program on a national network and a busy media center for sharing the gospel message.

Ten

Fall of the Dictator

"We've just been told a military coup is taking place." My colleague's voice was loud and agitated. "They are saying the prime minister has gone to the National Guard barracks downtown to try to organize a counterattack. We must close the office and go home until the situation becomes clear." A sense of alarm overtook the four of us in the office as we discussed the news. It was late April 1974, and we were in Portugal.

I picked up the office phone to call my wife at home. "It has to be a joke," she laughed at the mention of a coup. When I assured her that it was no joke, she suddenly became serious, "Well, please come home right away and be careful."

"Don't worry, dear. I'll hop on the next streetcar up the hill and be home in a jiffy," I replied. With one hand, I hung up the phone, and with the other, I reached for my shortwave radio. "If anyone can tell us what is happening, it will be the good old BBC," I told myself.

"Leading the news today is the latest on the apparent military coup in Portugal. For a direct report, we go now to our correspondent in Lisbon," said the newscaster.

"Here in Lisbon, there is relative calm, but the military, under the apparent leadership of General António de Spínola, has declared that the Caetano regime has been toppled, and the military is firmly in command, with the possible exception of some outlying barracks of the National Guard," the reporter explained. I stood transfixed, maybe just a few blocks from where the correspondent was stationed. He went on to say that the key to the situation was whether all the military would bow to Spínola's command or whether some would remain loyal to the old government.

All of a sudden, I realized that things could get ugly rather fast. Aside from personal danger, what concerned me most was that Radio Trans-Europe—the station that was broadcasting our AWR programs to Europe, North Africa, and the Middle East—might be forced off the air. Would the Lord permit this situation to silence His message?

Our office was not far from Eduardo VII Park, at the center of the city. Curious to see what was happening down at street level, I went out to the balcony of our office suite. Looking down at the cobblestone street, I spotted a green army tank at the corner. And just at that moment, two fighter jets flew low over the city. Otherwise, it was deathly quiet, save for the comforting sound of the clanging iron wheels of a streetcar coming from a distance down the street.

Rushing back inside, I grabbed my jacket and keys off the desk and headed for the door. Then I remembered the stack of mail on my desk. If I could just get this to the post office, maybe the postal service would be able to get it on its way before everything turned to chaos. The main post office was on my way home, so I bundled up the letters and Bible lessons.

"The police may not let us go all the way to the end of the line," the conductor informed me as I jumped through the streetcar's door. I noticed there were only two other passengers.

"That's all right," I replied. "I'll just go as far as you go."

The streets were empty of traffic. Usually a bustling, noisy city, Lisbon was as quiet as if it were a holiday. As we approached the central post office, more pedestrians were milling about. This was closer to the commercial center of the city, and I felt calmer seeing people out on routine errands.

I jumped off the trolley and strode across the street to the cavernous central post office. Just as I dropped the letters into the mailbox near the door, I heard *bang, bang, bang, bang*. Gunshots! I hadn't heard that sound since my army boot camp days.

Immediately, as if a film had been fast-forwarded, everyone in sight began to run. I did too. Around the back of the post office and down the narrow back street, I ran. Soon I was the only pedestrian on the street. Fortunately, by then, I was within a couple of blocks of the streetcar stop where I could catch a trolley up the hill to our apartment in old Alfama.

"This is the last *eléctrico* for today," the trolley conductor nervously said as I jumped breathlessly through the door.

"Great; I'm glad I caught you," I gasped.

After a half-dozen more people ran up to the car, it began its noisy, clanging trip up the steep hill to the beautiful old section of town.

When I walked through the front door of our little apartment, I was nearly knocked over by Andrea, who bounded at me to squeeze me with a giant bear hug. "Oh, I've been so worried. Why did you take so long getting here?" she demanded.

When I told her about my stop at the post office, she scolded me. "Don't you know it's dangerous out there? The radio keeps announcing that everyone should stay home until the situation is resolved."

"Oh really?" I said innocently. "Do you have any more news?"

"Come, our neighbors know all about it," she said as she led me to the back balcony. In Lisbon, the best place to get all the news was out on the balcony, where apartment windows looked out on the courtyard below. This is where the laundry was scrubbed and hung out to dry; it was also where all the women hung out to share family news and neighborhood gossip.

Sure enough, a half-dozen neighbors were sharing bits of information, trying to figure out the true condition of the government. Rumors were rife, and bits of news from the surrounding apartments revealed a rise to near hysteria.

"They say it should all be over by sundown," our next-door neighbor was saying to a lady on the next floor.

I interrupted their conversation to say, "I was just down at the post office and heard some gunshots. Do you know what is going on down there?"

"Oh yes, that is just a couple of blocks from the National Guard barracks where the prime minister has been corned by the army," she said. "You weren't really down there, were you?"

"I'm afraid I was," I said sheepishly. "But I ran for the last *eléctrico*

Fall of the Dictator

up the hill, and I didn't see anything of the army."

"You were lucky. Who knows what might happen down there?" Andrea scolded. She held my arm tightly.

"How are you doing for food? Do you have enough for a few days?" our thoughtful neighbor asked as a quick afterthought. "If you need anything, let me know. We have some things we can share."

Wonderful Portuguese hospitality in the midst of government collapse, I marveled. We assured her that we had plenty to keep us for a few days.

We spent the rest of the day inside the apartment, reading books and preparing meals. Every so often we would watch out the front window or go to the back balcony to see if any more news had moved along the neighborhood grapevine. We included a session of prayer, asking the Lord to remember His work during this time of trouble and protect Radio Trans-Europe from political interference so that AWR programs could continue undisturbed.

Thursday, April 25, 1974, the day of the great military coup, was soon history. The uncertainty about how things would turn out continued through most of Friday, but by the weekend, things had settled down. It was a weekend of celebration. City residents formed spontaneous motorcades through the streets, horns blaring, welcoming the change of government. Others were in a state of shock. What would the future bring? Another dictator? Would Spínola be true to his promise to permit democracy?

Andrea told me about a conversation she overheard on our street. "I've been a slave to this country all these years!" one man said. "I was afraid to speak out, even in my own family, because I never knew who might be an informer." Stories began to surface in the newspapers about blackmail, informers, and political prisoners during the dictatorship.

The country heaved a giant, collective sigh of relief when national radio announced that the prime minister, the country's former dictator, realized his days in office were over and surrendered to the Portuguese military. The coup became known as the Carnation Revolution because people in the city presented flowers, mostly red carnations, to the soldiers in the streets when they heard the news of the dictator's downfall.

"And listen to this," Andrea said as she read the special edition of *Diário de Notícias*, Portugal's main daily newspaper. " 'Only two people lost their lives during the two-day revolution. Two soldiers became victims during tensions in front of the central barracks.' That must have happened at the very time you were at the post office last Thursday!"

I winked at her and smiled. It was good to know my beautiful wife of three years was so concerned about me.

During the next few months, we agonized with the people of the turbulent country as they endured the vicissitudes of emergency conditions, the harangues of political upstarts, and the uncertainty of a new political future. Immediately after the revolution, political parties with all kinds of rhetoric surfaced. Communists, probably the most vocal of the parties, came in force to push for their brand of politics. Socialist, centrist, and royalist parties appeared overnight. The beautiful monuments and facades of Lisbon's handsome buildings were soon blanketed with political posters and graffiti.

The military junta, to its credit, was able to stabilize the course of the country until elections could be held. But the turmoil caused by the two-day Carnation Revolution would affect the country and its territories for years to come.

But for the moment, we were glad we could get back to the work of preparing radio programs. Our days eventually returned to a semblance of routine.

"We didn't lose one minute of radio time through the whole episode. We were the only station that wasn't ordered off the air," I telephoned church headquarters in Washington, DC. Our ability to maintain broadcasts straight through the revolution strengthened our resolve and faith that God was with us. It was a strong indication to us, among many that we were to witness throughout the history of AWR, that the Lord would jealously protect this special ministry so it could continue to search out His people in all corners of the earth.

Eleven

Trials and Triumphs

"You won't believe what I had to go through to get this bottle of corn oil," Andrea said with a hint of distress. She had obviously gone through an ordeal, for she seemed tired and irritated. Strange things were happening in Portugal.

"I asked for oil at several stores and was finally directed to a little shop down Blind Alley," she continued.

Blind Alley was the name we had given to a very narrow street a few blocks from our apartment in Alfama. It was only wide enough for one car or one streetcar to pass through at a time. When riding the streetcar, we could actually reach out the window and touch the building facades because the street was so narrow.

It was a place that every driver hated but had to use if he or she wanted to get to our section of town from the downtown area. City hall tried to help the situation by stationing two watchmen as traffic coordinators. Each had a paddle, much like a table tennis paddle, with one side painted red and the other green. Their job was to sit at the only spot where traffic from both directions could be seen and give the sign, red or green, depending on which way was clear.

It actually worked quite well unless one of the watchmen left his post for a few minutes, fell asleep on the job, or got embroiled in an argument as to who had the right-of-way. Then vehicles from both directions would enter Blind Alley, and at the middle, both would claim their right to pass. A snarling traffic jam would ensue, horns would blare, tempers would flare, and it would take hours to clear the alley. We learned to accept it as part of the color of old Alfama.

"Then I had to wait until there were no other customers in the shop to ask whether the clerk had any oil for sale." Andrea's voice brought me back to her story. "Then I had to assure the shopkeeper that I would become a regular customer at his store. Then I had to pay twice as much as normal for the oil. Then I had to wrap it in paper so no one could see it as I carried it out of the store," she said with finality.

"Well, you know it was the same way at the service station," I tried to console her. "The line of cars wound around the block. I had to wait in that line of cars for a full hour to get to the gas pump, and then the station attendant announced they sold out of gasoline, and I had to start the process all over at another station."

That was the way of life in Portugal in late 1973 and into 1974. People were short-tempered and irritable. Food shortages were common. We heard of hostilities in the overseas provinces of Angola, Mozambique, and Timor. It was this unrest that led to the Carnation Revolution. The euphoria of victory, however, soon turned into disillusionment, which was fueled by broken promises, and economic turmoil.

The previous government's financial support of the overseas provinces collapsed, and the military leaders' reaction to those provinces' drag on the Portuguese economy was to grant them independence. Thus, the world's last great colonial power relinquished its control over millions of people in Africa and Asia.

Suddenly, Lisbon and other cities in the country were overrun by Portuguese citizens from those distant provinces. They were called *retornados* (returnees). Many of them were business owners who were forced to leave their overseas jobs and homes, often with only the clothes on their backs. Bankers and businessmen became paupers overnight. Beggars began to appear in subway stations and on street corners in Lisbon—something rarely seen before the revolution. The city was filled with people wandering around in shock. Hotels were forced to take in the refugees for temporary shelter, and the rooms were paid for by foreign governments that were asked to help.

"Where's our car?" I asked out loud one Sabbath morning as we were

Trials and Triumphs

leaving for church. "I know I parked it on the other side of the street," I said in dismay as I looked at the empty space where I had left the car the night before. We quickly looked up and down the street, but the car was nowhere in sight.

We walked ten blocks to the nearest police precinct to report the missing car, then halfheartedly walked home to contemplate this latest dilemma. The police officer said we would be informed when the car was found. We thought, *But how effective will they be at looking for our stolen car?* Some of our church friends, when they heard of our predicament, said the best way to find a stolen car was to ask radio stations to announce it on the air, then listeners would be on the lookout and call the station.

Before the weekend was over, there were four sightings of cars fitting the description of our red Fiat—one of the most popular models in the city. But having no transportation, we had no way to follow up on the reports. A week later, a police station called to report that our car was spotted by a guard at a police post in midtown. The alert officer saw the car pass his post, and then he saw it parked in a nearby square. With the assistance of a colleague, he went to inspect the car and found a man sitting in the front passenger seat. The man was immediately arrested.

The car looked as though it was driven through the woods at night; it had scratches on both sides from the mistreatment. It was out of gasoline, and the key to the gas tank cap was nowhere to be found. I used a hacksaw to cut the locked tank cover. Then I hiked to a service station several miles away to get gas. When I returned, the car was gone! In dismay, I went back to the police again to report the missing car and then headed home to wait for any news.

"It's the police station; they found the car," said Andrea as she handed me the telephone when I walked in the door at home. "They say they found it abandoned in a square and had it towed to the main police station."

I immediately caught a taxi and went to the main police station to collect the car. We were glad to have wheels again, and with a fresh paint job, it looked like new. Several months later, I was summoned to court to witness that it was, indeed, my car that was stolen. The man the police found in the car was acquitted because they couldn't prove he was the man who actually stole the car; he claimed he was only a passenger.

Meanwhile, back at the office, we were celebrating the addition of two more languages to our broadcasts: Turkish and Norwegian. This brought the total number of languages to seventeen. Another funding crisis came at the end of 1974, but Walter Scragg was again given space in the *Review*, and donations picked up. Still, the outlook for 1975 was uncertain. Despite our concerns, the number of languages climbed to twenty in 1975.

In that same year, Andrea and I had the privilege of attending a worldwide event for the Seventh-day Adventist Church—the General Conference session. We planned to make broadcast reports from this big event in Vienna, Austria, for our station in Portugal and in local stations in different parts of the world. This meant we would be away for several weeks, so we obtained permission to hire an assistant named Manuel Vieira to fill in for us in Portugal. He was a young married man who was interested in learning the radio work. His talents and interests were such that he continued with AWR as a valuable employee for many years thereafter.

The church business session was held in the largest convention hall in Vienna, and many thousands of people from around the world were in attendance. One exciting aspect of the event was that, for the first time, delegates from Bulgaria were permitted by their government to attend. Also, a Russian delegation was there for the first time in forty years.

The session also held elections for church positions. AWR was affected when Walter Scragg was elected president of the Northern Europe–West African Division. M. Carol Hetzell, a longtime communication specialist at world headquarters, was elected director of the newly formed Communication Department, which included the church's radio ministry.

When it was time to return to Lisbon, Vienna's newspapers were reporting on the alarming politics in Portugal. They reported that clashes between the Communist Party and the rightist parties were at a fever pitch. The Communists were able to bring in land reforms in the agrarian south of the country, but the small landholders of the north, who felt they had already been independent for decades, resisted these reforms. More than just resisting, they attacked and burned down the Communist Party's headquarters in the northern city of Oporto. The press coverage of the isolated clashes in Portugal gave the impression that the whole country was ablaze. Relatives and church workers were concerned for our safety; some even wondered whether we should return to our home there. We returned to Lisbon, however, without incident.

In 1975, Radio Trans-Europe opened a new opportunity for AWR. The company was involved in a new shortwave station being built on the island of Malta in the Mediterranean Sea; it would give us excellent coverage of the Middle East. I was instructed to investigate the Malta prospect.

"I didn't want to arrive in Malta this way, by airplane," I wrote for the *Review* in the summer of 1975. "I would much rather have traveled by boat, like the prisoner Paul," I explained. However, to be on the island at all was a thrill, and I was especially moved when I visited St. Paul's Bay, where the great apostle supposedly landed with the passengers and crew of the wrecked ship, as recorded in the biblical story. It is also the spot where the apostle was bitten by a snake and miraculously survived.

The new radio station at Delimara Point had an impressive antenna array and a 250-kilowatt shortwave transmitter with good coverage of the Middle East. On August 1, 1975, AWR began broadcasts over this new station. But the added costs to the church brought financial challenges to the point where, at the end of 1975, we feared AWR might close down completely. But thankfully, the world church, especially leaders in Europe, came to the rescue and allocated new funds to the AWR budget.

While all of these events were taking place, I felt the need to return to the United States to continue my education. As an American army veteran, I was still eligible for financial help with advanced education under the GI Bill (a scholarship fund awarded to veterans who chose to return to college). But we were dedicated to the mission of AWR. The original one-year term had now stretched into five years, and we loved our work. We decided to ask for a one-year leave of absence. It would be enough for me to finish a master of arts degree.

"Here's a letter from church headquarters," Andrea said as she came into the studio where I was working several weeks later.

The letter stated that we were granted a study leave, with hopes that we would return to Europe in a year's time. On the recommendation of Willma and Olov Blomquist, Ron Myers, a popular gospel music announcer in Southern California, was asked to take our place for that year.

Our five years in Portugal had been exciting ones for us and for AWR. The radio ministry now seemed to be on a strong footing, and under Ron's leadership, AWR's future in Europe could continue to grow. As it turned out, his one-year appointment turned into a multiyear appointment, and our one-year leave turned out to be more than one year. But AWR would continue to be part of our lives for many years to come.

Twelve

A Stint in Local Radio

"Well, aren't you a pretty sight!" were my first words of greeting to my wife when I found her in the middle of the kitchen; hands and arms covered with applesauce. She had traveled to Andrews University in Berrien Springs, Michigan, a few weeks before me, and now she and Colleen Smith, a new friend, were deep in the busyness of canning.

"Yes, I'm a mess, but won't you be glad for this applesauce next winter?" was her quick reply. We learned that canning fruit and vegetables for winter was the universal summer activity for people in this part of the United States. Fruit was abundant, and canning supplies were readily available. After a joyous reunion, Andrea and I quickly found our apartment in the basement of a faculty member's home and settled in.

Soon I was so busy being a scholar again that I had little time to think of my AWR days or even radio itself unless it pertained to my academic media studies. I did visit the university's radio station, WAUS, a few times, and one thing that intrigued me was the station's use of a satellite dish to receive national programs. I began to think about what a godsend this new technology could be to AWR's mission to send God's message around the world.

In the long run, it is the heavy burden of creating programs on an hourly, daily, and weekly basis that can cause a local station to succeed or fail. A satellite distribution system eventually helped to spread the heavy load of program production over a network of stations. In 1995, the Novo Tempo radio network in Brazil became the church's first network to take advantage of satellite distribution of programming.

It was greatly satisfying to know that AWR had generated interest in radio as a major way to reach people in every corner of the world with God's message. Our shortwave broadcasts also demonstrated to the governments of Europe that Seventh-day Adventists had a message so important that we would develop any means necessary to accomplish our mission.

Graduation for my one-year study program was nearing when I was called to the university president's office. "Would you be willing to stay on at Andrews to manage our radio station? We will sponsor your advanced studies if you stay on and serve the university in this capacity."

We had a dilemma: we had promised to return to AWR after our one-year study leave.

We shared our dilemma with M. Carol Hetzell, the new Communication Department director at church headquarters. "Ron is doing a good job and is willing to stay," she replied a few days later. "You are free to stay at Andrews, just so long as you plan to return to AWR someday," she wrote half seriously. But my interest and love for AWR continued, and notes in my diary followed its progress. I constantly searched church publications for AWR news and even had the surprise opportunity to assist with AWR programs from WAUS.

In October 1976, the new AWR board approved broadcasts under the name *AWR-Asia*, aired over Radio Sri Lanka. The programs would be produced at the church's Poona (Pune), India, studio under the supervision of Adrian Peterson. The programming included his popular *Radio Monitors International* program.

In 1977, I had the privilege of meeting H. M. S. Richards again. He came to the Andrews University campus expressly to speak to theologians in training, but he also visited our radio studios one day. His vision for reaching the world with radio was as strong as ever. He reported that the government of Liberia was willing to grant AWR a broadcast license.

Pastor Richards's wit and wisdom enthralled the seminary students wherever he went on campus. I remember one of his comments more than others. When asked by a student what the greatest influence in his life had been, he said, "My wife, my wonderful wife." His campus visit was the highlight of the year, and although saddened by his passing a few years later in 1985, I felt fortunate that I had been given the opportunity to interview him.

Also in 1977, the General Conference Committee, meeting at church headquarters, accepted a long-range plan devised by the Communication Department to cover the world with the AWR signal. It would require three or four large shortwave stations.

Back in Portugal, Ron was pursuing every avenue to find ways to widen AWR's broadcast area. The success of AWR-Europe's programs, broadcast from Radio Trans-Europe, was increasing the demand to stretch AWR's signal to more distant places. Excited about the potential for reaching all the world, the Lisbon team—Ron and Annie Myers and Manuel Vieira—prepared a document that proposed stations in Madeira, the Philippines (with Guam listed as an alternative), Seychelles, and the Bahamas.

In a letter, Ron wrote, "Did you know that FM radio is exploding all over Italy?" I could easily read Ron's excitement between the lines. "Last year's test case against an Adventist businessman who was operating his own radio and TV station out of his house was won by the defendant. Now hundreds of small- to medium-sized stations are popping up on air without licenses and are perfectly legal. I counted 20 or more just in Rome. For $25,000 or less, we can plant a radio station in the heart of Rome!"

With help from the Blomquists and other friends, Ron was soon able to do just that—put an FM station on the air in Rome, originating just blocks from the Vatican. It seemed a miracle that such a thing could happen in Europe, where private stations had been forbidden for so long. Since that time, the station has had an incredible history of ups and downs, including the bombing of the studios, mysterious loss of equipment, and other tragedies, but today it's the flagship of a struggling but active network of local stations operated by the church in that country.

In time, I would have the opportunity to visit the station myself and present a training seminar there.

Italy was the first country in Europe to totally open up the airwaves to anyone who could broadcast responsibly, but soon other countries

A Stint in Local Radio

gave the same freedom: France, Belgium, Sweden, Norway, Denmark, and in the 1990s, Romania. Our people in those countries could write books about God's miracles on their behalf. One of the last countries to permit such freedom was Great Britain.

All those new opportunities proved the mettle of our church members. Usually, programs only went on air when individual church members were willing to make the personal sacrifices required to maintain the programming. This meant long hours volunteering, learning from their mistakes to produce quality programs, and struggling to locate resources. Those who volunteer today are still my heroes. In spite of little to no financial support from the organized church, they believe strongly in the church's mission to give God's message to their communities, and they make it happen.

Paolo Benini is one man who has done much for radio work in Italy. As a local pastor, he was instrumental in establishing several radio stations on the island of Sicily. When elected president of the church in Italy, he was especially proud of the radio station in Rome. Under his leadership, the station was able to increase its power and obtain a new transmitter and automation equipment, and the station became the church's best witness in the Eternal City.

Along with Ron's news from Europe came some disappointing news in 1977. While its big neighbor to the north was expanding individual freedom in places such as Rome, the government of Malta, a small island south of Italy, was objecting to AWR's plans to broadcast programs to Yugoslavia from Radio Mediterranean. The island's government was apparently getting pressure from all sides. Now they were edgy about their relations with Communist Eastern Europe. We had hoped this station would provide a way to broadcast to vital Eastern European nations and Arabic-speaking countries of the Middle East, but instead, we were only permitted to broadcast Western European languages. Ultimately, AWR ceased broadcasting from that station in 1982.

With the decreasing workability in Malta, Ron began investigating other possibilities in Europe. He found a small station in the mountainous country of Andorra, nestled between France and Spain, that would accept AWR programs. "With the booms of rocketing fireworks bursting outside the studio window, AWR-Europe's first-ever live broadcast began over Radio Andorra International," he later wrote about the momentous day of September 8, 1979.

"A hundred thousand or more visitors came to help the thirty thousand native Andorrans celebrate their national holiday. But few of the festivity makers were aware of another important event taking place at that same moment: the first AWR transmissions on this small but mighty three-kilowatt station nestled in the Pyrenees," he wrote.

Broadcasts from Andorra continued until the spring of 1981, when the government closed all stations in its territory. Concessions for private broadcasters to operate had expired, and the authorities nationalized all radio and television stations.

The AWR signal over Radio Trans-Europe remained strong, however, and its frequency became well established. Proof of its effectiveness came in the form of stories about listeners in Eastern Europe. In 1979, James E. Chase, director of the Communication Department at church headquarters, wrote in *Tell* magazine:

> A Hungarian man heard the *Voice of Hope* on his transistor set, and the truth went to his heart. He wrote Paris for the Bible lessons and went on to complete the course. Then there was silence.
>
> For two years, the Bible school did not hear from him. But the truth that had been transmitted into his heart was taking root, resulting in changes in his lifestyle and his relationship with Jesus Christ. As his life touched others during those two years of silence, he shared with them his wonderful newfound faith through personal testimony and Bible studies.
>
> Finally, the period of silence was broken by his request for the speaker of the Hungarian *Voice of Hope* program to come and baptize him and others. They all wished to do the Lord's will completely. Fortunately, the speaker was able to respond to the request. He examined their spiritual understanding and was so fully persuaded of their experience that they were not only baptized but soon the group was organized into a small church.

Heinz Hopf, communication director for the Euro-Africa Division, sent in another story:

> The place is a remote corner, a village not easy to reach, somewhere in Eastern Europe. The scene: Every Sunday morning, a group of about ten people meet in the home of family C, who

A Stint in Local Radio

possess a radio set, a rather old but good shortwave receiver. There they listen together to the *Voice of Hope* from faraway Portugal. Months pass. Finally, the pastor of an Adventist church decides to begin evangelistic activities in that area of his district. He mails invitations to all neighboring villages. By "chance," an invitation comes into the home of that family. Once they attend the first meeting and find out that it is the same message they have listened to on the radio, they do not miss a meeting. Through winter's ice and snow, they ride bicycles the ten miles from the village to the meeting place. Today they and two of their neighbors are preparing for baptism.

The year 1978 turned out to be a milestone in Adventist radio history. AWR had proven its ability to reach the unreachable. Church leaders set out a bold plan to encircle the globe with the Adventist message through radio. In the spring of the year, the presidential administrative committee decided to ask the church in its Annual Council to approve moving ahead "with a denominationally owned radio station in Liberia, Africa, as funding becomes available and a continuing study of programming by the Far Eastern Division for broadcast to mainland China and acquiring a new station in Guatemala."

One year later, in 1979, AWR-Latin America was born when shortwave broadcasting began from Guatemala. Bob Folkenberg, president of the church's Central American Union, realized that radio waves could reach far into the jungles and mountains of his mission's territory—Belize, Costa Rica, El Salvador, Guatemala, Honduras, Nicaragua, and Panama.

As for the effectiveness of radio, he told us of an experience that convinced him of its universality. Riding a donkey one day through drizzling rain in the forest, he heard the sound of music wafting down the hillside. Peering from under his poncho, he saw another traveler astride a donkey, coming down the muddy trail, carrying a radio. It was the sound of HCJB, "Voice of the Andes," a famous missionary radio station. He decided then and there what the Seventh-day Adventist Church must do, and he went on to found AWR-Latin America, later renamed AWR-Pan America.

In 1981, Mike Wiist was called to manage AWR-Europe when Ron Myers left to manage two stations of his own in France. A decision was made to build a small shortwave station at Forlì, in northern Italy, in the expectation that the government there would soon make private broadcasting legal.

In late 1983, church leaders agreed to sponsor an hour a day in French on Africa's most powerful radio station—Radio Africa No. 1—in Gabon. But the matter of pulling together a professional team to produce programs was a challenge.

One day at my WAUS office, I received a telephone call from Tulio Haylock, an associate director of communication at the General Conference. "We have signed a contract for AWR to start broadcasts to Africa, but we don't have a studio or staff where programs can be produced. That will be organized soon, but we need programs right away. Would you be able to help us out with this?"

Knowing that Andrews University had students from around the world, I agreed to pull together a team of French-speaking students to do the job. Soon we had a team of four graduate students—three of whom were actually from French-speaking African countries—who, with a little training, were writing and voicing the first programs for AWR-Africa. I was glad that God had placed me there at that time when a new chapter of history for our church in Africa was launched.

My graduation at Andrews was nearing, and I was anxious to return to the world of international broadcasting. I prayed that I might be needed again by AWR because it was the most exciting prospect I could imagine.

Thirteen

Asia Calling

"This is the day I've been working toward, but I sure do wish it was already over," I confided to my wife. It was the day of the big test—the oral defense of my dissertation. I was confident in my preparation. Many people told me, "If anyone knows this subject, you should, after all the months of study and research." I think it's what they tell everyone who has pre-exam jitters.

"A Model for Development of a Telecommunications Satellite Network for Administrative, Educational and Other Purposes in a Private Organization" read the front page of my defense. The name was so long I could barely remember it, but it looked impressive, and I secretly hoped the technological aspects of the topic would intimidate the examining committee enough that they would take it easy on the questioning. The use of satellites for communication purposes was an emerging technology at the time, but I was certain it would one day become a fact of everyday life.

The examination session lasted several hours. The six professors grilled me one after the other. I found myself actually enjoying the opportunity to defend my topic—one that I fully believed would advance the cause of God for the church. It would be a new, inexpensive way to distribute radio and television signals to broadcast stations and even to churches, schools, and hospitals. If nothing else, I hoped the university would be willing and proud to have it lined up with all the other dissertations on a special shelf in the James White Library.

A number of friends requested permission to attend my defense, and before I knew it, they were hugging me and patting me on the back as the dean introduced me as "Dr. Steele." My mother was visiting us at the time, and I was happy to see her beaming smile at the back of the room.

With my diploma in hand, I was now ready to go out and serve my church in a broader field again. It was time to contact Bob Nixon, the new communication director at the General Conference. I told him I was available if AWR needed me, and I hoped I could once again be of use in sharing the good news with the world. He said he would share this news at church headquarters and get back to me.

A few weeks later, I was looking out the window at snowdrifts that reached nearly to the roof of our house and the neighbor's house. The telephone rang. It was Bob Nixon. "We've just received a building permit from the Federal Communications Commission to install a radio station to broadcast to all of Asia. Would you be willing to head up this project?"

"Did you just say the 'Federal Communications Commission'? That means it will be on US territory, right?" I was flabbergasted and tried to think. *Where does the United States have a territory close to Asia?*

"Yes, it will be on the island of Guam, a US territory in the western Pacific. And thanks to God's guidance and the help of George Jacobs, we've been able to obtain US permission to put a shortwave station on the island, and we're anxious to start building," he continued.

But I barely heard what he was saying. My mind was already racing through the work required for a move to a tropical island in the Pacific Ocean. I did a double take at the name of George Jacobs, however. He was famous as the chief engineer for the Voice of America for many years. Because he was the foremost authority on broadcast engineering, I was acquainted with several of his articles on his specialty of short-wave propagation.

Jacobs lived in a suburb of Washington, DC, and Maryland, and now as a consultant, he had his office in downtown Silver Spring, Maryland. In the search for engineering expertise for the huge AWR-Asia project, Tulio Haylock contacted attorney Don Martin, an Adventist church member who practiced communication law, to ask whether he could recommend a broadcast engineer who could serve the church as our consulting engineer. His recommendation: George Jacobs.

When George was contacted, he said, "Oh, I know you Adventists well. Our Jewish group in suburban Maryland was looking for a place to have our Sabbath meetings several years ago, so we contacted your church. We received permission to have our meetings in the lower-level chapel of the Sligo Seventh-day Adventist Church."

He readily agreed to help prepare the station application and represented AWR at the Federal Communications Commission (FCC) during the lengthy approval process, which began in April 1984. The result was the expedient granting of a construction permit within a surprising six-month period. He then continued to advise our station staff with spectrum analyses when the station became operational. (A spectrum analysis determines the best frequencies for broadcasting to specific countries.) George became a most valuable member of our team.

"Welcome to paradise," said Linda Bauer, the Guam-Micronesia Mission president's wife. Her husband, Bruce, was away on a trip, so she came to welcome us with flowers at the airport at four in the morning! We soon learned that most flights arrive in Guam during the dark hours. Airlines from Japan, Korea, the Philippines, and even the United States made their schedules to accommodate the departing city, not the arrival city of Agana (now Hagåtña), Guam. Many flights from Asia to the island are second duty for airplanes that fly during daylight to major cities and then return to their home bases at the end of the day. They are then used for a rather short hop across the western Pacific to Guam.

The plan worked well for the airlines, and Guam's hotels were constantly preparing rooms for quick turnarounds to accommodate the new customers who were arriving sometime during the night. They quickly filled the rooms of guests who had left earlier in the evening. By doing this, they had more than 100 percent occupation rates.

People on flights from America arrived with their internal clocks scrambled from jet lag. From Hawaii, our flight took seven hours and crossed the international date line. So we left Los Angeles in the late evening, changed planes in Honolulu, lost a day when we went over the date line, and arrived at four in the morning. We had no idea what time it was or what day it was. But we were happy for the warm welcome.

We soon learned that Guam is one of the most welcoming places on Earth. Any excuse is used for a get-together or fiesta. Any event serves as a special occasion—weddings and birthdays, of course, but even a baptism, new building, new office, or new home. A rule of thumb for the host and hostess is to prepare twice as much food as you think you'll need so that all will marvel at the bountiful spread and there will be enough left over for those who linger on and need another meal later in the day. This spirit of hospitality has made it a major vacation destination for Asians who wish to experience a bit of America close to home.

We were eager to see the site where the station would be built. To find a property large enough to build a sizable international station on such a small island had to be a miracle. The island is thirty miles long and twelve miles wide at its widest point. With a land area of only 212 square miles and 116,000 inhabitants, where would there be room for a multi-acre radio station?

Tulio Haylock, associate director of the church's Communication Department in the 1980s, was instrumental in locating a spot for AWR's large station for Asia on the island of Guam after searching all over Asia.

Haylock spent many months, we learned, looking around Asia for a place to establish an AWR station that could reach all the countries of Asia. He visited Korea, the Philippines, and the islands of the Pacific, searching for an appropriate site. Finally, all the factors needed to successfully build and operate a radio station focused on one place: Guam. As a US territory, it would be a safe, politically stable island to build and operate a facility such as the church had in mind. But was there land available?

Haylock's best helper in the search was Ray James, communication director for the church in the Far Eastern Division. He previously had been president of the Guam-Micronesia Mission and knew the island well. While searching for property on the island, he discovered a large tract of land that was for sale on the southern part of the west coast.

It was just south of the town of Agat on a point of land called Facpi Point, which jutted out into the Philippine Sea. It was an ideal spot for aiming a powerful radio signal across the sea to the countries of Asia.

"And the land was without form and void," Andrea paraphrased Scripture when I saw the property on our first visit. I saw on the map that the plot was on the extended slope of Mount Lamlam—Guam's highest mountain at 1,332 feet above sea level. Scant vegetation covered the area, and large patches of eroded red soil marred the terrain, making one section look like a miniature Grand Canyon. The land was owned by members of the Torres family. It had been divided by the Torreses' father in his will into equal portions for his several children.

We set out to tromp through the field to determine where property boundaries were located. This was a challenge because the saw grass was high, the sun was hot, and the land was very uneven. One could easily fall into a hole or ditch with just a slight misstep.

"Do you see what I see?" I asked the group that joined me for the initial inspection. We had been tromping half the day, measuring the distances from one palm tree to another.

"We don't have access to our land! We'll either have to build a bridge over the river and build a long road to the highway or buy some adjoining land so we can have a direct road to our property from the highway." The final decision was to see whether we could buy more land.

"How will we ever erect large curtain antennas on this hilly place," I murmured to myself. Some ingenious planning would be needed. A critical piece of the puzzle would be to gain the approval of local authorities to purchase and develop the land. We would have to submit a building plan for approval, obtain permission from all government departments, and hold a public hearing for local residents in Agat.

The project also presented a financial challenge. The General Conference Committee agreed to allow the station to be the recipient of the official offering to be taken at the General Conference session that would be held in New Orleans in the summer of 1985. We had to wait to see whether the entire project, costing an estimated $5 million, would fit into the funds that would be raised at that event. There would also be a worldwide offering day for the project when all Adventist congregations around the world would be invited to support the project with their offerings.

As usual, God's timing was perfect. The offering was taken just as we began to build the station, and we eventually had the privilege of dedicating the facility debt-free, thanks to the generosity of God's people.

As for additional land, three lots of about six acres each, owned by three sisters of the Torres family, abutted the twenty-two-acre plot we had already agreed to buy. Our abilities would be challenged. We would not only have to find a place in our budget for the additional property, but I would have to dip into the Torres family politics to convince the sisters to sell their land—their inheritance. The Torreses were a charming and interesting Chamorro family. Delicate diplomacy would be needed.

The family patriarch had subdivided the land at Facpi Point into thirty-acre plots so that each son and daughter would receive an equal amount for their inheritance. They, in turn, subdivided their plots into equal amounts for their children. The additional parcels we were seeking to create a right-of-way to our station belonged to three of the granddaughters.

I wasted no time in making contact with the three sisters. Two sisters were quite willing to sell their land for a good cause, but the one who owned the middle lot was hesitant. She was thinking of her son and wanted to save some land she could leave to him in her will. My negotiations with her stretched over several months.

As a busy businesswoman, the only time she could see me was during her breakfast hour at Linda's Café on the beach at Agana Bay. Over a large glass of orange juice, I discussed the possibilities with her. Reluctantly, she finally agreed to sell most of her lot if a small plot, large enough to build a house, could be reserved for her son. While it was not ideal for our station's needs, it was the only agreement we could make that would satisfy her.

With the land issue solved, the next step was to petition the local government for permission to build. First, our plans had to be approved by the Department of Land Management so that the property could be rezoned from farmland to light industrial. This involved several sittings with the Land Use Commission at their weekly meetings.

Next, we had to schedule a public hearing so that local citizens could give their approval of the project. If we were to be successful in getting this final clearance, we knew we would need to do a good bit of public relations.

"I'm glad we have a public relations director on our AWR staff," I said to Andrea as I opened our planning meeting. The AWR board vice chair, Lowell Bock, had made sure Andrea was elected to serve as the public relations and program director for the new facility. She was known for her talents while at Andrews, where she served as public relations director for the university.

"Well, since we are the only two people on this committee, we should be able to come up with a plan," she answered when I outlined the challenge before us. "First, we need to let all our church members in Guam know about the public meeting planned for June 19, 1985. Some of them have contact with government officials, and that will be helpful to us," she added.

"We also need to try to gain public approval. Maybe some newspaper advertisements will be the best way to do that." It was obvious she had already been thinking of a plan for smoothing our entrance into the local community.

We immediately started planning to purchase four half-page ads in the *Pacific Daily News*, the island newspaper, then owned by the Gannett Company. One ad would tie us in with our large medical clinic on the island, another would identify us with the Guam Adventist Academy, a third would link us with the vegetarian restaurant operated by the mission, and a fourth would clearly show we were associated with the Adventist churches on the island.

The day for the public hearing arrived all too quickly. The municipal building in Agat is a low one-story building located right at the water's edge in the heart of the village. Agat was known for its beautiful ocean-side location and its backwoods area on Mount Lamlam's slope at the rear of the town, which was the only place on the island where deer roamed freely in the tropical forest. The beach was also a place for sailboarding and diving, and the town was known for its cockpit at nearby Nimitz Beach, where weekly cockfights took place.

The mayor's office was in the municipal building, next to the public meeting room where our hearing was to take place. Mayor Tony Babauta was 100 percent behind our project. He became a great friend of AWR and was always asking how he could help. His support was crucial to our success.

At the appointed hour, officials from the Territorial Planning Commission arrived to join the mayor for the hearing. I was the first speaker, and I presented the scope of our project using maps and graphs to indicate the type of facility we planned to build.

A representative from the US Navy rose to speak. "We have concerns about this station and its radio waves. We fear those waves could interfere with our highly sophisticated communication systems on our ships at the base, just a few miles away at Apra Harbor."

I was able to respond that in our license application process in Washington, all US military departments signed off on our application. So that possible conflict had already been addressed. "Thanks to George Jacobs," I whispered under my breath.

We learned after the hearing that a second objection came from another shortwave broadcaster at the southern tip of the island. Even though they had no representative at the hearing, their lawyer had written a formal objection to the FCC in Washington. Fortunately, their letter arrived two days after the FCC granted AWR a license!

The officials continued to discuss our plan among themselves, then turned to the twenty or so people in the audience. As I looked across their faces, I noticed a large majority of those were Adventist church members. To our surprise, the chief land commissioner asked each person to state whether he or she was for or against the project. Person by person, the project was approved by the group. There were fifteen votes in favor and four abstentions. There were no negative votes.

Now that we had all the permissions that we needed to proceed, we could turn our attention to other urgent matters, such as getting an architect for the building, finding an equipment company for towers and antennas, ordering transmitters, and finding the programs that we would need when we went on air. We prayed, "Lord, just a few more miracles, please."

Fourteen

Pulling It All Together

A crew of about twenty-five people would be needed to build the Guam station, and we had to bring all the elements together at the right time. An engineering team, who would install the towers, antennas, and transmitters, needed to be employed; an architect and construction company had to be brought on board; and the programs needed to be produced. These three facets of the project would keep us busy.

Our first order of business was to bring together an engineering team who would decide what equipment to use and get it installed. We found that our chief engineer on the island, Butch McBride, had worked on a large shortwave station on the neighboring island of Saipan and a similar station on Guam after coming to the islands from California.

Our assistant chief engineer would be Don Myers, whom we had met at Andrews University, where he was heading up an affiliated industry on campus called the Electronic Design Company. The third engineer would be Brook Powers, whom I had hired as an assistant engineer at WAUS. When I told him about the Guam project while he was still a student working at the university station, he seemed to take my suggestion that he would be needed on Guam as a joke. But he eventually agreed to join us and ended up being one of AWR's long-term employees.

Once we had the engineering team in place, we were ready for them to set about their task of bringing together all the technical aspects of the station. The station complex would sprawl out over nearly thirty acres of the hillside at Facpi Point. The antenna fields would take up most of the space with four antennas in two arrays—one for northern Asia and the other for southern Asia. The supporting towers would be three hundred feet high, and the antennas would be suspended between the tops of the towers. During the construction phase, the engineering team would hire local teams of ten to twelve laborers to assist in the gigantic task.

Meanwhile, I started to search for a local architect to design the building, following a floor plan that I devised. It would have ten thousand square feet of space and house more than $3 million worth of equipment. The building would have a large transmitter hall, a control room, and a second wing to house a production studio and offices for administration, programming, and public relations staff. A basic staff would include directors of the departments and volunteers to accomplish the duties. We immediately put in requests to the Adventist Volunteer Service for veteran retirees and student volunteers. During our seven years in Guam, we welcomed a score of university students and a dozen seasoned retirees.

Buildings on Guam must be constructed to withstand typhoon winds of up to two hundred miles per hour. To strengthen the structures, poured concrete roofs and cement-filled block walls are standard. At our facility, self-sufficiency would be of utmost concern, so a rainwater catchment system and standby generators would also be needed.

A building permit was obtained from the local government, but several delays were encountered—rain, the navy, and a hill! Locals told us that summer was one of the wettest seasons they had seen in recent years. We needed at least five days of dry weather before we could risk using bulldozers for earthmoving. The island was drenched with fourteen inches of rain in one month, August, just when we were ready to start clearing the area.

At the last moment, the US Navy claimed to be uninformed about the AWR project and raised questions again about AWR's radio signals interfering with aircraft and ammunition facilities. They asked the planning commission to delay granting a variance request on the property until they could research the matter more thoroughly. The commission gave them a week to respond with an official ruling. They came back with confirmation that the navy's headquarters in Washington had, indeed, already approved AWR's permission to proceed.

There was also a small hill in the path of our access road. Some local residents said they thought it was an ancient Chamorro landmark. At our request, the archaeology section of the Department of Parks and Recreation sent a team to inspect the hill. Their research concluded that it was not of historical significance; its most significant use was by a Japanese gun crew during World War II.

While construction on Guam proceeded, Andrea and I set about searching for program content in Asian languages. We soon learned that the church's Hong Kong–Macao Conference had a radio production studio where programs in Mandarin and Cantonese could be made. They were able to rent time on local stations in the area, but the stations were not able to penetrate very deeply into China. They were excited about the prospect of being on the new AWR station on Guam, which would reach the mainland.

For some time, Adrian Peterson had been working hard in India to build up the church's production to make programs in Hindi, Marathi, Telugu, Malayalam, Tamil, Bengali, Kannada, Urdu, and Sinhalese, which are the major languages spoken in that country. A major production studio would be established in the city of Poona, where these programs could be recorded.

On a visit to Thailand and Burma, we discovered small studios in Bangkok, Thailand, and Mae Sariang, in the north of Thailand, were producing programs in Thai and in Karen—the language of the Karen people. In Burma (later named Myanmar), there were no radio programs, but church leaders were eager to produce programs and obtain their own studio to reach the twenty million people in that country.

Andrea visited studios in Yokohama, Japan, and Seoul, South Korea, where programs were already being produced for local stations. The main target of the Korean *Voice of Prophecy* was to reach into North Korea and Manchuria, where many Koreans live. There were also programs being produced in the Philippines and Indonesia. But new studios and training would still need to take place in Bangladesh, Sri Lanka, Nepal, Vietnam, Cambodia, Laos, and possibly Papua New Guinea.

With these commitments for program production, we began building a program schedule that would start in May of 1986. More languages would be added, but we had a good schedule to start with. Now everything depended on the engineering and construction teams to complete their parts of the project.

In late 1985, we received word that the federal government had given our station an official name. Stations east of the Mississippi River have call signs that begin with a *W*. Stations west of that river have call signs that begin with *K*. It seems Guam was considered west of the Mississippi. We learned that a station had recently given up the call sign KSDA, so we requested it for our new station. It was granted, and our official identification came to be "Adventist World Radio, KSDA, Agat, Guam." As a result, the little village of Agat would become a household word for many.

Our engineering and construction teams continued to be confronted with various problems: "He says we can't make our road through his banana trees," Don Myers, our assistant chief engineer, said in dismay as I walked up to the bulldozer. We were finally ready to start grading a road to our building site. We assumed we would be required to follow the map made by the government surveyor, but a nearby farmer discovered that the route went right through his small banana plantation, and he was not about to let us mow down his trees.

"Let's talk to him together and see if we can't work something out," I said as we turned to where the farmer was standing like a sentry at the edge of his garden.

The towers for the Guam station were hoisted and bolted together, one by one. Eventually, seven towers supported five antennas; each was the size of a football field.

Pulling It All Together

"You can see here on the map where the access road is to be built," I tried to explain. "It's the only place the government will let us grade for a road."

"That's OK, but it will take down a whole row of my best banana trees, so it's not OK, you hear," he rejoined, quite agitated. This was not a good start with our neighbor, and we were the new kids on the block.

"All right, we'll leave the row of banana trees, but we'll put the road just to the right of your line of trees and hope we're not too far off the mark for this entry road," I suggested.

"That's OK; I'll go for that," he smiled. It seemed like we had made a good friend, and our crew spent the next two hours digging up pepper plants and small banana plants to transplant to an area our new friend indicated behind his house. Several months later, the farmer's wife, Maria, came to work for us as a custodian at the station. She quickly became part of the AWR family.

The Guam-Micronesia Mission had a couple of empty offices that we were invited to use for the summer months, but as the season waned, we had to find a new location until the new building could be occupied. And we needed to be closer to the building project.

I approached the owners of homes at the south end of Agat, nearly in sight of our construction site. "Excuse me, would you happen to know of anyone who wants to sell or rent their house in this area?" I asked.

At the third house, I was greatly encouraged. "Well, I've heard that the young woman across the road there wants to sell her house." The man pointed across the street at a little pink stucco house. "She's just started working for Congressman Ben Blaz in Washington and needs the money to buy a house in DC." As a US territory, Guam is permitted to have an elected nonvoting member in Congress. Citizens are also permitted to elect the island's governor and legislature, but by federal law, they are restricted from voting for the president of the United States.

I thanked the man profusely and hurried to call the number he had scribbled on a piece of paper. Soon AWR became the owner of what forever would be known to us all as "the pink house." Over the course of nearly two years, it served as our office, and it was broken into by thieves three times. A stray dog adopted us—we named her Lady—and she became our watchdog until she was stolen one night. Occasionally, a huge sow came around the house in the heat of the day, and several times a hefty water buffalo came to peer at us through the windows.

In some ways, the enthusiastic interest in the Guam project made progress difficult. There were people so taken up with the excitement of the project that they felt possessive of it and us. One man, expecting that he would be asked to head up AWR-Asia, went so far as to call all the public utility agencies on Guam to inform them of our needs, ostensibly for the project. I discovered this when I made my initial contact with the power, water, and telephone companies.

"Oh yes, someone called us on this, and we sent them the information," they told me.

But at the same time, praise the Lord, thousands of people were solidly backing the new station with their funds. We were delighted to hear that the General Conference offering total was close to $4 million. Although we still needed another $1 million to finish the station, the treasurers predicted that amount would come in as donations during the next year.

Adding to our excitement, we were informed that Neal C. Wilson, the president of the General Conference of Seventh-day Adventists, was initiating a campaign for an endowment fund; the interest from the fund would provide an annual budget to operate the station. Within a year, $4 million had been pledged for this special fund, and it grew until it topped $5.5 million in 1992.

We were humbled to be part of such an important activity for the church and so grateful for the outstanding support. How important it is, we concluded, for missionaries to know that the folks back home are solidly behind them, praying and paying so the Lord's work can advance to the farthest edges of the earth.

At the construction site, heavy rain kept causing difficulties. "The rain won't stop," our chief engineer complained. "It will take us forever to get this done at this rate." The rain problem became part of our daily conversation with the Lord. We kept reminding ourselves that this was His project, and He would see that it got done.

One of our lowest points came one day late in 1986 when we had scheduled a special cement pour at tower base 1. Nine truckloads of cement were on order for an early morning delivery. The trucks were late in arriving, and at midday, a steady downpour commenced.

All afternoon the lead truck attempted to drive up the hill to the pour site but could not make it through the mud. We got a bulldozer

Pulling It All Together

to try to pull the truck up but without success. Finally, the engineers tried to carry the wet cement from the truck to the base site at the top of the hill and were able to fill some anchor holes but not fast enough to guarantee even half of the cement would make it to the top before it hardened in the mixer trucks. Finally, much of the cement had to be poured out onto the ground, and delivery was rescheduled for a better day.

Every day had its victories. We rejoiced when we saw the foundation of our building finished. It required 128 cubic yards of cement, delivered by sixteen large cement trucks. The walls seemed to go up quickly. The roof pour, on August 19, 1986, was thrilling as 350 tons of concrete were spewed out of a cement pump truck that looked like a giant elephant with an extralong trunk.

Next came the enormous yet exciting job of setting up the offices. Furniture, cabinets, appliances for the kitchen, and production and on-air broadcast equipment were all part of the move-in project. For our office staff, the installation of two new Macintosh computers—some of the first on the island—was especially exciting.

As for the outdoor installations, the antennas included thousands of parts that had to be assembled by hand. There were fifty galvanized steel anchor rods and twenty-six thousand pounds of guy wire cable. The towers came to Guam in four forty-foot containers. Altogether, the two giant tower-antenna systems arrived in forty-thousand pieces. While the concrete bases were being prepared at the tower sites, the towers were being constructed on the north side of Agat at a twelve-thousand-square-foot warehouse rented by AWR.

The logistics of the project were staggering for our small crew. The days were long, hot, tiring, and always hampered by tropical rains. But slowly, things took shape, and we began to have a vision of what our station would look like. By mid-1986, our hopes were soaring, and we felt a growing optimism that would fully explode by the time of the scheduled inauguration on January 18, 1987. The date was set, and all efforts were directed toward that deadline. But in the back of our minds, we were all asking ourselves, *Will we be ready?*

Fifteen

The Trumpet Sounds

"Well, we're only a week away from inauguration, and we still don't have an antenna ready or the road to the building paved!" Our new treasurer, Marvin Baldwin, was sharing his thoughts out loud. We were all feeling the jitters of the last-minute squeeze to get everything ready for the big event. Church leaders had their flight plans, and the office of Guam's governor reaffirmed his participation in the ceremony.

We also invited the Voice of Prophecy choir from South Korea to sing for the ceremonies, and they raised their own airfares for the trip. A brass ensemble from Guam's Adventist churches had been practicing for many months for the occasion. Several of Guam's mayors and senators were invited.

For the fiesta meal, we asked for the help of Mariquita Taitague, the wife of Pastor Frank Taitague. Mariquita was known in the local church as Guam's hostess par excellence. She and an army of church members were planning a lavish display of the island's cuisine for the event.

Two days before the big weekend, the road pavers showed up with their full complement of equipment. The road wound from the main highway, Guam Highway 2, through the flattened "Machine Gun Hill," down to the station property, through the former mini–Grand Canyon, and then up to the AWR building. The paved road was beautiful and

The Trumpet Sounds

The grand opening of the Guam station was attended by Seventh-day Adventist Church president, Neal C. Wilson (left). The author stands between Wilson and Governor Ada of Guam.

finished the station site in a most spectacular way. Now everything was ready. We made it!

At the ceremony, recently elected Governor Ada praised the church for its accomplishments in Guam, especially in matters of health and human life. He further wished AWR success in its "mission to bring a message of hope—a promise of a better tomorrow—to millions of people yearning to be free."

General Conference President Neal Wilson said, "A long-cherished dream is fulfilled, and many fervent prayers answered." Andrea and I gave each other a knowing look. We knew it was not only the dream of those of us who had been called to work directly on the project, but church leaders and members around the world had been dreaming of this day for a long time too—and they had provided financial support to make it happen.

After the speeches, we took the governor on a tour of the station. We were proud of the large L-shaped building. It was bright and functional. The large transmitter room was designed to accommodate two more transmitters in the future. The entrance, featuring a long, permanent canopy for protection from the rain, was situated at the center of the building. Glass windows gave visitors good views into the studios and master control room. Skylights down the long hall of the administrative wing made the building bright even without lights. The roof was designed to serve as a catchment system to collect water in a large tank at the rear of the building.

After the tour, the governor rejoined Neal Wilson at the front of the building, and together they went through the fiesta line to start the meal. We were anxious to expedite the governor's visit because we had been told that he could not stay long. We were surprised when he stayed more than an hour after the meal, just chatting with Pastor Wilson.

Our staff was exhausted after the big events surrounding the inauguration of the physical plant. We were disappointed, however, that we were not yet on air. But work continued on the erection of antennas 1 and 2. One person who was determined to see the antennas go up was Reinhold Grellmann, a student missionary. Even when our engineers were off the island on other business, Reinhold worked overtime to get the antennas up so we could start broadcasting. He epitomized the twenty-five young workers who came during the seven years we were in Guam. Without them, we could not have progressed as rapidly as we did.

The student missionaries worked in engineering, operations, programming, public relations, and many other areas as needed. Most of them took a year out of college study to gain practical experience at AWR. Working conditions were not always pleasant. In fact, they were nearly always challenging, but the student workers bore the situation

At the grand opening, the AWR staff decided to raise a flag for every country reached by the Guam station. Ever after, it was a tradition to display the flags on special occasions.

well and contributed greatly to the launch of AWR-Asia.

Our staff members shouted with joy, hugged each other, and cried tears of happiness when test broadcasts began on our two first transmitters at 2:35 P.M., Guam time, on March 5, 1987. Calls made to Hong Kong and Singapore verified that the signal was, indeed, being received in those locations. Regular programming began at 7 P.M. on Friday, March 6, just as the sun was setting on the rim of the Philippine Sea. Church workers from the Guam-Micronesia Mission, the Guam Seventh-day Adventist Clinic, and the Guam Adventist Academy came to witness this historic event and rejoiced with our AWR staff.

The first reception report arrived the following Monday from a young listener in Japan. By the end of the month, more than one hundred letters had arrived from twenty different countries, including Japan, Korea, Hong Kong, Singapore, China, Malaysia, Indonesia, the Philippines, Australia, New Zealand, Italy, and the United States.

We read each letter with profound excitement:

"I'm very pleased in sending you this report. I've been waiting for this day for a long time. Congratulations on the birth of AWR-Asia."—Japan

"A good, clear signal most of the time . . . very best wishes for great success with KSDA."—Australia

"Looking forward to some interesting programs from you!" —New Zealand

"What a thrill it was to hear the words, 'This is KSDA, Adventist World Radio-Asia,' and to hear 'Lift Up the Trumpet.' This is what I have been praying and working toward for many years—to see the church proclaiming the gospel to the world with a *loud voice*!"—Texas, USA

"I am pleased to inform you that the AWR-Asia broadcast reaches me clearly in North Sumatra, Indonesia."

"Thank you very much for your broadcast. I am not a Christian, but I enjoy your English program. I promise to continue listening to your broadcast."—Japan

One of the earliest success stories was from the country of Burma (now Myanmar). In response to the broadcasts, our studio in Rangoon (now Yangon) began receiving scores of letters from most of the seven states

Church group in May Lwin's village who witnessed God's power when the poison didn't kill her. May stands holding her child in the middle of the photo.

and seven municipal divisions of the country. The church's communication director wrote, "Listener letters are coming from areas where we have never visited and have no church members, and requests for the Bible course comprise almost half of all mail received!"

One man in Burma wrote that he had organized a group of eleven people to listen to the broadcasts every day—his family. "My nine children are aged 22, 20, 18, 16, 14, 12, 10, 8, and the youngest is 6 years old," wrote the forty-three-year-old businessman. He closed his letter by asking AWR to "please enroll" them in the Bible correspondence course.

A teenager wrote to say, "I am not a Christian, but after listening to your broadcast, I enrolled in the Bible correspondence course." He was eager to report that he had found someone to study the Bible with him—his brother, who was a Buddhist monk!

A Burmese police officer named Chin was baptized in early 1989 after hearing our broadcast from Guam. During a period of disappointment in his life, Chin heard the station theme song, "Lift Up the Trumpet," on his portable radio. He said the song made him forget his anger. He wrote to request the Bible course, completed the course, and was baptized.

Church headquarters in Burma were quick to follow up on the early responses. One young Adventist, a former national wrestling champion, headed out to a new area. Even though he was not gifted as a public speaker, he was sent to a mountainous area where Adventists had never been before. His only tools for his work were a Bible, his guitar, and a shortwave radio. His strategy was to go to the town square and start singing songs with children and others as they gathered around to hear his songs. He would then read some Bible texts.

To close the performance, he would turn on his radio and invite everyone to listen to AWR. His efforts were very successful, and several new church groups developed in that area. Other dedicated young people, most of them graduates of the theological seminary, were sent to areas where new groups were forming as a result of the radio broadcasts. Church leaders said dozens of new churches were established in this way.

At the invitation of listeners in a village where there were no Christians, members of the radio production team from Yangon (formerly Rangoon) held evangelistic meetings in May of 1990. Four people became church members—the nucleus of a new church group. The next year they again held meetings but this time in the capital city of one of Myanmar's states. Seven people were baptized to start a church group in that city.

Probably the most incredible story to reach us from Myanmar was that of a young lady by the name of May Lwin, who lived in a remote part of the country. She listened to our programs from Guam on her father's battered shortwave receiver and decided to enroll in the Bible course. She soon became a Christian, the only one in a village of spirit worshipers.

But "the Evil One" was angry. A villager, jealous of May Lwin's happiness, appeared at her home one day to pronounce an evil curse on the family. May's parents demanded that she renounce Christianity lest they all suffer a great calamity. But she refused.

They then demanded that she leave the family. Desperate in her desire to follow her new faith, she sought the only way out that would keep her faith intact and maintain the respect of her parents: commit suicide by taking poison—an acceptable act among her superstitious people.

Her family prepared to mourn her demise, but to their amazement, she did not die. A second time she took poison, but she didn't die. Such a thing had never before happened in her village.

"She serves a powerful God. He did not let her die after taking the poison," her father said in stunned amazement. "I must let her worship as she wishes," he declared to the villagers. Soon a new Adventist church was built in her village as a witness to the power of the true God and the young lady who wouldn't die from poison.

Sixteen

Island Life and Beyond

With our island family of workers and volunteers, the Adventist presence on the southern part of Guam grew significantly. Before we arrived, through the persistence of a little lady by the name of Jelly Macadagum, a small group of believers started meeting on the back porch of her house in the Agat suburb of Santa Rita. The group grew until about fifty people were attending. Needing more space for worship, they rented a Sunday keeping church in the center of Agat. When our AWR group arrived, it was obvious that an even larger meeting place was needed.

Our team soon found itself not only building a radio station but also a church. We purchased a property just off the main street of Agat, and on Sundays, our staff could be found working in the hot sun, digging and pouring the foundation, then constructing the walls of a handsome new church that would seat one hundred. Early on, a field was planted with watermelon seeds, and the sale of the fruit paid for much of the building materials. It was a grand occasion when finally, after two years, we proudly participated in the building's debt-free dedication. It was the fourth Adventist church on the island and the first with air conditioning. It became the spiritual home for our AWR staff for many years.

Island Life and Beyond

Other than enduring eternal summers, life on Guam among its hospitable inhabitants was a delight. "Guam's social life can't be beat," boasted our new program director, Greg Scott. He joined us from Europe, where he had been the manager of a station operated by Ron Myers in the South of France.

Those of us with AWR not only had the joy of serving the church during the week but also on weekends. For myself, my concern was that young people be given a high priority in the church. I decided to get back into the Pathfinder Club business. Activities in the great outdoors soon became a favorite pastime for the young people. Guam is a jungle paradise and weekends were often devoted to camping in the jungles or at the beach. Such activities allow for closeness between the teens and the club leaders, providing opportunities for counseling and encouragement during difficult times in the teens' lives.

Together we climbed mountains, stood under waterfalls that plunged from cliffs, and swam in underground pools in dark, cool caves. We were constantly warned of the prolific brown snakes, supposedly brought to Guam on cargo ships from the Philippines during the Second World War. During my seven years on the island, however, I only saw a couple of the creatures, and they never interfered with our camping expeditions.

In the evenings, around a campfire, I liked to read the true story of an isolated soldier to the campers. During the Second World War, the soldier was a radio operator who constantly relocated in the jungle to avoid enemy discovery.

Another true but utterly amazing story that took place on the island of Guam was the saga of another soldier who hid out in the jungle for quite a few years. During the Second World War, the island was occupied by the Japanese. They fortified the island against attack, with the heaviest defenses along the western coast from Facpi Point, now the site of AWR-Asia, to the village of Tamuning on the north of the island. The US Armed Forces landed on Guam on July 21, 1944, and secured the island after several weeks of fighting.

Fear of being captured by the US military drove Shoichi Yokoi, a twenty-nine-year-old soldier, into the jungle. He refused to surrender; to do so would have been highly dishonorable. He lived with two other soldiers in a cave near the inland town of Talofofo. They ate coconut, taro, soursop, freshwater shrimp, and eels from the Talofofo River. They fashioned shrimp traps from bamboo, made rope from coconut fiber, and clothing from wild hibiscus.

After thirteen years, the two other Japanese men moved to another cave; they later died in the jungle during flooding. Yokoi dug another cave about seven feet underground in the middle of a thick bamboo forest. There he lived until 1972—twenty-seven years after going into hiding!

One evening two Chamorro men were out hunting in Yokoi's vicinity. They spotted a moving figure in the thick bushes. With guns in hand, they ran after the figure and knocked him down. They were surprised to see that their prey was a thin, wild-haired, and even wilder-clothed Japanese man. "He had clothes like the skin of a tree, . . . he was scared; he thought I was going to shoot him," said Manuel de Garcia, one of the hunters.

Instead, he was taken to officials who learned his amazing story through an interpreter. Yokoi was then repatriated to his homeland, where he became a hero and a wealthy man, due to his army back pay of nearly three decades of wages. He and his wife were subsequently guests of honor at ceremonies to dedicate a replica of his cave at the beautiful Talofofo Falls Park in Guam. At that time, Yokoi, then seventy-one years old, said he still considered Guam his second home.

Guam was also a second home to thousands of military personnel stationed at US Navy, US Marine Corps, and US Air Force bases; about a third of the island was occupied by military personnel when AWR arrived. Some of the most desirable places for Pathfinder outings were on military property, and we found the base commanders were quite willing to permit well-supervised youth groups to experience the wilderness areas of their domain.

A popular spot for us was Ritidian Point on the northern tip of the island. From there, we could see across the ocean to the island of Tinian. (During the Second World War, Tinian had a large airbase from where the huge B-29 bombers took off to the north to bomb the cities of Japan.) But Ritidian was one of the very few places one could experience cold temperatures: it was in the waters of a small cave next to the ocean shore. The trip along the coast to the cave was a challenging hike but worth the effort when we squeezed through the tight entrance down into a room where a four-person-sized pool of frigid water waited.

The delights of the island came to their climax at Christmastime.

Island Life and Beyond

Eliyas Subakir *(right)* studied the Bible with F. J. Wuysang *(left)*. As a new believer, Eliyas went on to found a church that soon had one hundred members. This area of Indonesia was on the Global Mission list of one million people where there were no Adventists—until AWR was heard there.

That's when dozens of young college students arrived on Guam from other islands of the western Pacific for the holiday. At that time, the Seventh-day Adventist Church had the largest private school system in the Micronesian islands, and Adventist university students from the US mainland were recruited as volunteer teachers at the schools. They were encouraged to have airline tickets not only to their assigned island but also to Guam. This way, once during the year, they could enjoy the wider amenities of Guam before going back to their assigned schools, which, in many cases, were on much smaller and more remote islands with fewer places to eat, shop, and relax. Guam was the "big city" of America's Pacific island protectorates.

While those of us involved with the AWR station project were pleased to be part of such a huge undertaking, there was one major drawback. Our Guamanian friends frequently let us know that they were proud that their island was chosen for this project, but at the same time, they were sad that the radio programs broadcast from Agat could not be heard on the island of Guam. The shortwave antennas were aimed at the ionosphere above the earth to bounce down at the distant target areas of Asia. Guam itself was not part of our coverage area.

I sympathized with our local friends. While church leaders were on the island to dedicate the shortwave station, I asked them about the possibility of setting up a station just for Guam. Our church president encouraged the idea and said he would help find funds for the project. Soon AWR resources and personnel were stretched for the construction of a local station. On April 17, 1990, the FCC granted a construction permit for a 3-kilowatt station, KSDA-FM, on Guam.

In 1991, we had the privilege of celebrating the start of the station we identified on air as "Joy 92"—a name suggested by Greg Scott, our program director. We hoped that someday more of the isolated islands of the Pacific might have a local station to call their own.

Meanwhile, the AWR shortwave station continued to reach all of Asia, and new groups and churches were beginning to spring up in many places. By ones, twos, and more, people were finding our shortwave frequencies carrying the message of hope they were longing to hear.

A man walked into the Kamenokoyama Seventh-day Adventist Church in Japan, where an evangelistic meeting was beginning, and registered with the receptionist. When asked how he learned about the meeting, he said, "By radio." When questioned further, the man said, "Yes, it was by radio. I am a faithful listener of the AWR Japanese programs."

One day in February 1989, in the Indonesian village of Sarirejo, a forty-seven-year-old farmer named Eliyas Subakir turned on his radio and heard AWR's broadcast in Indonesian. He was amazed to hear about the Adventist belief that Saturday was a holy day and a day for rest. He began to study the matter in his Bible, and he became convinced that the Adventists were right to believe as they did. Soon he was the leader of a group studying this new faith.

In the spring of 1991, Eliyas and his wife joined thirty-two others who were ready for baptism into the Seventh-day Adventist Church. Later in the year, their group grew by twenty-four. Most of the group were former Muslims or Hindus. The new church in Sarirejo was formed in the heart of the 10/40 Window—a global mission area where Adventists had no believers before.

A teacher in the Philippines wrote to say how useful the AWR broadcasts were to her. She used the things she learned from the radio programs in her classes.

In Indonesia, a religious leader, who especially appreciated the family-life programs in Indonesian, urged her parishioners to listen to the AWR broadcasts. She said that the programs were excellent and that she took thoughts from the programs and adapted them to her work as a family counselor and church leader.

An Adventist pastor in the North Solomons Mission of Papua New Guinea wrote to say he personally knew of another church in his village that heard the Adventist message every Sunday through their pastor, who was an AWR listener. That good man listened intently to AWR, then made up his sermon notes based on the broadcasts.

From North Sumatra in Indonesia, a listener wrote, "There are four families of us that always listen to your station, and we hope to promote it and invite our friends to listen."

A physician making visits to remote villages in the Philippines reported that in several places, groups of people gathered to listen to AWR on what sometimes was the only radio in the village. In one village, a man hooked an amplifier to his radio so the rest of the village could hear better! A letter from our program producer in Cebu, Philippines, confirmed the report: "Last week, a couple from northern Cebu came to my office to bring a 200 pesos donation for the radio ministry." He wrote, "They said, in their village, they are the only ones who have a shortwave receiver, but they are sharing it with their neighbors by connecting it to a powerful amplifier. As a result of this sharing, a company of believers is now meeting in their home."

In India, a Hindu man with a family of five said, "Through the Tamil programs, my family has come to know Jesus as the true, living God. We realize that idol worship is sinful, and we have repented of our sins. We hope to be baptized soon!"

An evangelist in a Pentecostal church in the same country wrote, "I have a congregation of 50 people. To feed them spiritually, I listen to the AWR Telugu broadcast and take notes, then I share the message with my people on Sunday."

"The AWR Telugu programs help me make the right decisions," wrote a young man. "I encourage my friends to sit with me to listen to AWR, and at least a dozen of them enjoy the programs regularly."

In Papua New Guinea, Joe Morgan was known by his friends as someone who could "drink alcohol like a fish drinks water." As a supervisor at a giant copper mine, he worked long days, then stopped at a bar for beer and staggered home to his apprehensive family, who feared his abusive language.

One day he staggered into his home and turned on his radio to hear the news. What he heard was the best news ever heard by man—AWR sharing the good news of salvation. Listening became a habit, then one Saturday morning Joe announced to his family that they were all going to church! Soon they were enjoying the church meetings at the Rumba Seventh-day Adventist Church in Arawa. It wasn't long before the love of God's family convinced Joe to give up his liquor, betel nut, and cigarettes, and a baptismal date was set.

Only a few weeks before the planned baptismal day, a medical checkup revealed Joe had cancer and little time left to live. On his deathbed, Joe earnestly told his wife and six children, "I have no regret. I have made my choice to follow the Lord. Be faithful to the Lord, my dear ones, and I'll meet you in heaven."

His wife and three teenage children were soon baptized, and at the funeral for Joe, many of his relatives indicated they would like to study the same Bible that had changed Joe's life so dramatically.

In Indonesia, a young man named Augustinus listened intently to AWR day after day at his home. As he studied the Bible lessons sent to him, he began to understand the commandments and more about Jesus' saving sacrifice. He said he felt he had been "far away from God." Then he met an Adventist pastor who began to study the Bible with him.

"I told my younger brother about these studies, and he joined me," he reported. Both young men were baptized. "We faced difficulties with our family and relatives. I am sixth, and my brother is the seventh in our family of twelve sisters and brothers. Please pray for us in our new faith."

Andrea and Allen Steele stand in front of the completed AWR-Asia building in Guam, 1989.

Island Life and Beyond

Fighting God seemed to be a way of life for Takuya in Japan. He wrote,

> I attended a Christian church when I was in high school. Then, during my college days, I forgot about God, and life didn't go too well. At one point, I even contemplated suicide. Only listening to AWR kept me from doing that.
>
> Then I started attending church again, but often found myself arguing with the pastor about the beliefs I learned from AWR. I started searching for the true church and ended up visiting about 20 different Christian churches. Then one day, God led me to the Seventh-day Adventist Church. I suddenly realized I had found what I had been searching for and was baptized on May 26, 1990.

One evening in Indochina, Mr. Maung was scanning his radio and was startled to hear a program he had never heard before. The reception was excellent, and the program was in his native tongue, so he continued listening. Later that evening, he told his wife how much he had enjoyed the program and said the station announced they would have another program in the morning.

Up bright and early as usual, the couple tuned in and sat listening to their radio. Through music and story and Scripture, the gospel message opened up to them. That night after supper, Mr. Maung gathered his children to listen. They especially liked the children's story.

It became a habit—early in the morning and in the evening—month after month, with conviction growing all the time. Finally, he wrote to the address given on the program, and the family began Bible studies. A year after, he wrote again to the Bible school and declared that he and his whole family were ready to become Christians through baptism. He was assured that a pastor would come as soon as possible.

But the "soon" became later, and when the pastor finally arrived, he found the family already rejoicing in their newfound faith. "We told our friends about our intention to become Seventh-day Adventists," Mr. Maung said. "Some people came from another church and urged us to join them. But we told them we believed that the Adventists teach the Bible truth and we would wait as long as necessary to join that church."

"I came to be baptized," another young listener in Indonesia announced at the Bible school in Jakarta. Zentua, twenty years old, came to Jakarta, Indonesia's capital city. He was determined to find the people who had been sending him the Bible lessons he learned about from AWR. He went on to explain that he had completed the Bible course and had been listening to AWR for some time. The Bible school teacher began to question him about what he had learned and why he felt he was ready for baptism.

The wise teacher soon discovered that Zentua, indeed, was ready for the important step into God's kingdom but that a few weeks of further study would be valuable. Two months later, he was baptized and began his new life as a Christian book salesperson.

Meanwhile, another young man arrived in Jakarta to enter the university. He knew no one in the city and was anxious to make friends. He decided to go to the only "friends" he knew in the city—the people at the Bible school whose address he had been hearing for three months over AWR. To his surprise, he met a friend from his hometown there—Zentua. It was a joyous reunion that became a celebration not long afterward when Marasati was also baptized into the church with Zentua at his side.

But this story has more than one good ending. One day Marasati's family summoned him back to his village because his parents had become seriously ill. He returned to nurse them back to health but also shared the story of his new, happy life. He encouraged everyone he met in the village to listen to the AWR broadcasts that came in so loud and clear on the radio. It wasn't long before his family was ready to be baptized, too, becoming the nucleus of a new church congregation in that town.

As for Zentua, he went on to study theology at an Adventist college and became an Adventist pastor.

Seventeen

Touching Hearts in China

The Guam station's primary target was mainland China, and we had good evidence that we were achieving our goal. During the first forty-five months that AWR was broadcasting from Guam, more than fifteen thousand letters arrived in response to our Chinese programming. In 1989 alone, just two years after going on air, six thousand letters had arrived from that great country.

Not only did we receive letters but more than half of those who wrote enrolled in the Bible correspondence course. Based on the mail received, we estimated that 80 percent of our Chinese listeners were young people.

We were also told that groups of people, large and small, came consistently to listen together to the radio messages on our station. University students seemed especially eager to form groups who would listen to the broadcasts. Weekend study classes were formed, and requests for Bibles constantly came to the Bible school. Adventist pastors were frequently surprised to find visitors in their congregations who heard the message on the radio and came in search of Sabbath keeping believers. Overall, these people had a deep understanding of Seventh-day Adventist doctrines and were more than ready to become church members because they had listened to AWR for many months before making a solid decision to follow Christ. Some listeners who accepted the Adventist message became self-, or we might say, God-appointed preachers.

A unique innovation for Chinese broadcasts was developed by Richard Liu, who succeeded Carl Currie as director of the Seventh-day Adventist radio production studio in Hong Kong. He developed the concept of a "College of the Air" and asked the Southern College of Seventh-day Adventists (now Southern Adventist University) in the United States to send a religion professor to help with the on-air classes. In response, Douglas Bennett, from the university's religion department, traveled to Hong Kong to record the programs as a cohost.

In a remote western city in China, a young American woman sat listening to the college class on her radio. "She was sent by a Christian church to teach English at a university school of economics," wrote Douglas. "She began to listen to the broadcast—a class on public speaking—then she listened to classes on Revelation and Christian beliefs. She got some Muslim students to listen with her, and now some of them are believers." His story also included the report of this young woman's baptism on November 26, 1994, on the campus of Southern College in Tennessee while she was on a visit to the United States.

"Recently, through the radio waves created by God," wrote a twenty-one-year-old in Shanghai, "I have been able to listen to your high-quality programs. They have helped me to know Jesus Christ, and now my heart is always filled with joy. I am going to do everything to follow Jesus with you. To help me, a seedling, to grow, please send me a Bible."

"I always listen to your broadcast," wrote another listener who worked in a chemical factory in Shandong. "Your programs are like rain watering my dry heart, giving me strength to go on. Although I am physically sound, I am spiritually empty and in desperate need of spiritual support. Under such circumstances, your explanation of the Bible brings me to a land of great happiness."

"I am a faithful listener of your radio station, for I enjoy your programs very much; the speakers have become my good friends and teachers," wrote a listener in Guangdong. "You are the lighthouse that pushes me to go on, helping me to face reality and live with determination, helping me to believe firmly in God. I have chosen the brightest path in my life, the way of God."

Another wrote, "I am a regular listener. Not long ago, I found your station accidentally. In the past, I did not have any religion, but after listening to your programs, I gradually have begun to believe in God." He had some good news to share as well: "I recommend your programs to my friends, and many of them have come to like your programs and will become faithful believers, I am sure."

University students revealed their search for meaning in life. A medical student wrote, "I was especially delighted to hear your program last night because it was my birthday! I plan to become a faithful listener. My classmates in the dormitory also enjoy your programs and are the ones who told me about them." Another medical student said, "In my class, twelve out of twenty-four students listen to your programs." He added an important note: "Four of them are women!"

From another city, a student wrote, "Every night I join my friends in the dormitory as we gather around the radio to listen to your program."

Another student, having failed to pass the university entrance examination, was ready to give up. He said, "My expectations turned into bubbles; my life became so empty that I lost faith in myself. Yet, while I was sinking into deep sorrow, I came into contact with your broadcast. Your voice was like a flowing stream, melting the ice in my heart and lighting a fire of hope. I continue to listen to your broadcast every day."

In 1990, an international news service reported from China: "In recent months, students have been converting to Christianity in large numbers." (We at AWR already knew this.) "The rate at which students are turning to Christ is literally a dormitory at a time."

On Christmas Eve 1990, the Adventist congregation in a certain city had planned a special Christmas celebration. As the members began to sing Christmas carols, something unusual happened. The church doors opened, and in came a group of university students—dozens of them! They had first heard the name of Jesus on AWR, and they were thirsty for words of hope. They wanted to learn about Christ, the Savior of the world.

The church elders put their heads together and decided to alter their program so the young people would hear the complete story of Jesus. The simple sermon was transformed into an evangelistic meeting—and what an attentive audience! Many of the students expressed a desire to study more and continued to attend that church regularly.

At another place in China, the only audible sound in the broad expanse of rice fields ripe for the harvest was the soft sound of a scythe against the rice stalks. But a voice was heard in heaven. While bent over in the rice paddy, swinging her scythe rhythmically through the ripened grain, Mrs. Wong constantly prayed that someone would send a pastor to her village in Manchuria.

She and many other families in the village listened to a shortwave radio to keep in touch with the world—a world so different from their quiet farming town in Northeast China. And the programs they listened to were all different too. News, sports, politics, and religion all vied for attention. But there was one program they kept returning to: it was in their native tongue, and the words of the speaker and the ideas he presented were new, exciting, and filled with hope. It was a program from AWR.

The Lord answered Mrs. Wong's prayer. One day a friendly and interesting man walked into her village. He went directly to a certain home, as if he knew the address, and after a time, he came out, accompanied by Mrs. Wong's smiling neighbor. After stopping at the house next door, they came to Mrs. Wong's house.

"Hello," the cheerful man said, "I understand you have written to the Bible correspondence school. Many of your neighbors did too. The school sent me here to teach you more about Jesus. I am Pastor Lee from the Bible school in Seoul."

And so it was that in one of the adobe thatched-roof houses, connected to each other in long rows for coolness in the summer and warmth in the winter, the Adventist message was spoken out loud for the first time. Mrs. Wong joined her other joyful neighbors for the first Adventist church service in her village. During his first visit, Pastor Lee baptized seven people. Some months later, he was able to return for seven more baptisms.

In another city, Mrs. Kwan, an AWR listener, asked her son and daughter-in-law to take a letter to the Bible school in Seoul when they visited South Korea. The young couple were not Christians but learned about Christian beliefs while staying with their Protestant relatives in Seoul. When they took Mrs. Kwan's letter to the Bible school, they were given a tour of the school, church, and adjacent hospital. They also signed up for Bible studies. Within weeks, they became believers and attended the church located next to the Bible school.

The time came for them to return to China. A baptismal ceremony was organized, and afterward, they were showered with gifts: clothes, books, and radios to share with their neighbors back in China. Pastor Lee from the Bible school accompanied them on their return trip and stayed on to teach others in their village. As a result, the mother of the newly baptized couple and six others became believers. These nine people continued to share their newfound faith and became charter members of a new church company.

Another story came to us about Mrs. Bao. One day she was sitting next to her radio with her pen poised to write down texts and thoughts that impressed her—a habit that began when she discovered the AWR signal from Guam. On this day, though she did not know it, she would hear something that would forever change the way she worshiped—she would hear about the Lord's true Sabbath.

Already a Christian, Mrs. Bao was astonished. She began to study her Bible and became more convinced. But she was still confused: Why did so many people go to church on Sunday if Saturday was the true day of worship? She decided to talk to her pastor. He told her that the day "had been changed," and now Christians kept Sunday "because Jesus was resurrected on that day." She wasn't convinced by his answer because she had been studying the subject on her own in her own Bible.

She returned home to study more and to listen to her radio. Finally, convinced beyond doubt, she realized that she would have to accept Saturday as her Sabbath by herself, even if no one else did. So she observed Sabbath in her own home by herself. But she became happier and happier as she continued to listen to AWR. Soon she had to share her discovery with others—her neighbors. Before long, ten people were meeting in her home on the Saturday Sabbath. She wrote: "Please send us an Adventist pastor to baptize us. We are ready."

Richard Liu wrote us about a most unusual thing that happened in another city. "The newspaper reports that a huge traffic jam occurred in the city last week." He found the strange story in a major Chinese newspaper. "It was an inconvenience to the people of the city, and the city fathers were not happy with the situation," he continued.

"The reason for the traffic jam was that one thousand people were being baptized in the river!" It was an Adventist baptism, he learned upon further investigation. "And we weren't even aware that there was an Adventist church in that city," he added.

Richard investigated and, a few weeks later, came back with the rest of the story: "We found out that several pastors from another location had traveled to the city to help baptize this large group. But city officials would not permit them to hold the ceremony because they were from outside the city, so the pastors ordained a number of local elders. It was these local church leaders who baptized the people who had learned about Adventism from listening to AWR." But the most surprising part of the story was that "the newspaper didn't want to emphasize the event," and the article was very conservative on the numbers who were baptized. "The elders say it was closer to two thousand people who were baptized!"

Our AWR staff in Guam were thrilled to hear of so many people in China listening to the broadcasts. Nearly two years of hard work and struggle through the driving rain in the red mud of Facpi Point had finally resulted in these days of reaping. Not only was the Guam signal finding new people who were longing for an encouraging message, but many former Adventists rediscovered a beautiful message from across the ocean: Their brothers and sisters had not forgotten them. The AWR broadcasts reminded them that the world family was alive and well and longing to help them grow and reconnect.

One letter brought news of a small home church where twenty to thirty people met on the front lawn. The owner told of his personal revival ignited by the AWR broadcasts: "I learned of the Sabbath when I was eight, and now, I am fifty-seven." There were nine families in his small village; five of them professed no religion. "Other members of our home church have to walk a long way to worship with us. The closest person walks for one and a half hours, and one family walks for four and a half hours. We are very happy to hear your broadcasts. We read the Scripture and sing hymns with you."

Another story came from a Chinese American Seventh-day Adventist who wrote to tell us he recently made a long-awaited and much-anticipated trip to his homeland to visit relatives in a large city in China. Though his relatives were not Seventh-day Adventists, they were sure they knew where an Adventist church was and readily agreed to take him there on Sabbath. Arriving at the church, they found the doors locked. A neighbor said that the church services were only on Sundays. Disappointed, they turned to leave but saw a large group of people approaching. Noticing that the group's leader had a Bible under his arm, they asked, "Are you Christians?"

"Yes, we're Seventh-day Adventist Christians," he replied. "Our church doesn't have a baptistry, so we have arranged to have our AWR baptism in this church." The visiting American and his relatives joined the group inside and watched as nearly two hundred people were baptized—another result of AWR's outreach from Guam.

A woman in a different city wrote, "I am a preacher in a large church. I think it would help me if I took your Bible correspondence course." We sent the lessons, but the Bible school got no reply for many months.

Then one day, a large envelope arrived. It contained the answer sheets for all the lessons she had received! Her enclosed letter also had many questions. These were answered one by one. She felt compelled to share the good news of her newfound faith. Later she established a new Adventist church in her home.

A young man in rural China listened to the broadcasts and recognized them as being from the church he belonged to as a child. His heart was warmed, and he decided he must be baptized. He took the train to Shanghai, a two-hour trip, to find an Adventist pastor. He was informed that no baptismal ceremony was planned any time soon in Shanghai.

"Maybe if you go to Beijing, they will have a baptism," suggested the pastor. The young man spent several hours on the train to Beijing. But again, he was informed that no baptism would be held until the next month. "But I can give you the address of a pastor who can baptize you any time," said the elderly pastor.

Again, he boarded the train for a trip to a Beijing suburb. When he arrived at the address he was given, he told his story to the elderly gentleman who came to the door. He was questioned about his beliefs, and he showed the pastor his referral letter from the pastor in Shanghai. The man then took him to his backyard, uncovered a tub that was hidden in the ground, and baptized him. This young man later left China to study in the United States. When he returned to Asia, he came to help AWR make programs for his people.

Another report told of a Protestant pastor in China who decided he should attend an Adventist church to find out why one of his most faithful church members had become an Adventist. As he spoke with the Adventist pastor after the church service, new spiritual insights opened before him. Convicted by God's Spirit, he realized he, too, must follow this new religion that made such sense for his life.

He returned to his home church and started preaching what he had learned. Many of his church members soon became Adventist believers. The numbers continued to grow until six congregations asked to be organized as Adventist churches. He wrote the pastor who had originally introduced him to this new religion, asking for another worker to come to help him lead the six congregations.

"We have a preacher for you," came back the reply. "He comes to us, too, every Saturday morning. We listen to him and are greatly blessed. You can hear him, too, if you listen to AWR. We have dozens of big and small churches that have no pastor except the *Voice of Hope* on AWR!"

When we started broadcasting to China in 1987, the church headquarters reported 21,168 members in the country. At the end of five years, with no help from the world church other than the AWR station on Guam, church membership grew to over 115,000. Radio had proven itself to be a powerful way to bring thousands of new believers to the Lord and nurture them to maturity in the truth.

Eighteen months after commencing broadcasts to China from Guam, there was another country we knew we were reaching with a good signal, but we hadn't heard from anyone there: Tibet. Finally, a letter came, and it was one of the most beautiful we had ever read.

"From your programs, I have learned some English," wrote the young woman. She was a worker at a weather observatory. "I enjoy your programs very much. It brings us closer. I dedicate this little poem to you and wish you a happy New Year." Enclosed with her letter was another sheet with this handwritten poem:

> From the clear blue sky, through the pure white clouds,
>   Slowly the melody reaches my ears.
> I hear your voices from the far side of the ocean,
>   At the same hour each day, we come together.
> The wave of sound brings blessings across the ocean.
>   Oh, radio waves, may you accompany us across the
>   endless years.

Eighteen

Storms out of the Blue

"Living on a small island, you're a victim of the sea," our neighbor Joe said one day. He was a product of the island of Guam, a native Chamorro, and he was always sharing bits of advice and wisdom with me from his store of folklore and island tradition.

The island of Guam is nothing more than a volcanic peak surrounded by coral flats. Just to the north is the Mariana Trench, with the deepest known valley of any ocean floor. Guam is the largest of the Mariana Islands and has become the commercial center for people in the western Pacific. It is the transportation hub for about a dozen airlines that fly in and out of the Pacific.

Because of the mountains in the south, the island has some sparsely inhabited areas. A number of streams, called rivers in Guam, pour out from the mountain peaks and tumble down into the ocean. One of my favorite hikes follows the Sella River up the southern hump of Mount Lamlam, the island's highest mountain, within view of the AWR radio station, to the river's source.

At every corner, water gushes through huge boulders to form small pools, some large enough to jump into and get relief from the stifling heat. Then the water hurries down another series of rocks to splash into the next pool. At the source, near the top of the mountain, water comes seeping out of the earth amid dense undergrowth. It is the sweetest, most wonderful water I have ever tasted.

One can easily get lost in the tall saw grass and jungle terrain on the mountain's flanks. Once, while on a hike with our Pathfinder Club, I noticed one lad was missing. Quickly, I turned back to look for him, calling his name as I walked down the trail. "I'm here; I'm here!" I heard a voice in the distance. He had taken a wrong turn and was struggling to find the main trail in the six-foot-high grass when he heard me calling.

Joe's idea of islanders being victims of the sea seems especially true during typhoon season when the storms roar across the western Pacific. They usually form southeast of Guam between the Marshall Islands and the islands of the Federated States of Micronesia, just north of the equator. Typhoons then take a convoluted path to the northwest, often headed for the bigger land masses of the Philippines, Japan, or mainland Asia itself.

The Micronesian islands are of no consequence to these giant storm formations as they trundle across the Pacific. It makes no difference what island lies in their paths; they just churn along, making twists and turns as a matter of course. The US Joint Typhoon Warning Center is usually able to give several days' warning when one is approaching. This gives people time to get supplies, board up their windows, and tie down anything that's loose around their houses. Airlines send their flights to safer places, and all ships move away from the area as fast as they can.

When landfall of a storm is imminent, everything on the island shuts down. The residents hunker down in their homes to wait out the storm. With gusting winds often reaching over one hundred miles per hour, anything not bolted or tied down is hurled through the air and can be lethal to anyone out in the storm. Coconuts become cannonballs and can cause bodily harm.

The storm is not the worst part of the trauma. The aftermath is what brings mass depression to people. Electricity is out because power lines are down, cutting off the pumps that distribute potable water to all the towns. Often, the government must send water trucks into areas where no water is available.

In 1991, Guam was visited by Typhoon Yuri. The Joint Typhoon Warning Center gave plenty of early warning, but the storm moved slowly in our direction, and the waiting became tedious. Finally, at nightfall, the siren winds started whistling around our house. During

A sailor on a merchant marine ship leads a Bible study
with the crew while crossing the Pacific Ocean.

the night, we opened our window a crack to get fresh air, but the noise kept us awake. It sounded as if a never-ending freight train was passing just outside our window.

Needless to say, such storms can cause damage to a radio station. During these storms, the glass insulators on the antenna are usually the first to break. Then the giant antennas must be lowered and repaired, which is an arduous task, requiring many hours of work.

During AWR's first ten years in Guam, no typhoon or earthquake was able to keep the station off the air for long. The worst damage occurred when Typhoon Omar made a surprise attack in August 1992. Winds gusting up to 154 miles per hour forced water through the station's cooling system and into several transformers, causing them to arc and burn out. After the storm, replacement parts had to be ordered from the US mainland or, in some cases, made by hand by our engineers. That took the station off the air for three weeks.

On August 8, 1993, the strongest earthquake in eighty-four years hit the island. It measured 8.1 on the Richter scale. The west end of the AWR building sustained moderate structural damage. Large cracks developed in the wall, big chunks of plaster fell off, and some of the concrete blocks in the wall were broken. The program tape library was in shambles. Thousands of cassettes were shaken off their shelves and smashed to the floor. But even in that upheaval, the station only lost seven hours of airtime.

Being out in the middle of the ocean as we were, helped us to understand a bit of what it must be like for sailors traversing the high seas. We received many letters from people on ships: military and merchant marine personnel and passengers.

"I have no religion, but to soothe my loneliness and the tediousness, I listen to your broadcast. I'll be going home in five months. Your programs will help me make it through," wrote a Korean sailor.

Another sailor, one of our church members from the Philippines, was the radio operator on a large container ship. He asked the captain for permission to air the AWR programs over the ship's public-address system. He was able to help his fellow sailors ease their loneliness by listening to the broadcasts in their own languages—Ilocano, Tagalog, and Cebuan. Soon ten crew members were joining him for regular Bible studies with the blessing of the captain, who appreciated the cooperative attitude his men had been displaying since they started listening to the programs. Two of the ship's officers and several of the sailors became church members at the end of their tour of duty.

"Remember Zhi Ming?" Andrea asked me one day, eyes dancing. "He chose a sailor's life. On board a cargo ship sailing the South Pacific, he found time in his off-duty hours to listen to his shortwave radio. He listened to the Mandarin broadcasts from Guam and became convicted that he should follow the Lord.

"Since he made that decision, he has found many ways to share his faith," she continued. "A fellow sailor, Chong, who was living a totally dissipated life, joined Zhi one day to listen to a tape of hymns recorded off the radio program. The hymn that caught Chong's ear was 'The Ninety and Nine,' and he was touched by the effort the shepherd went to, searching everywhere for one lost sheep.

" 'Could God love me like that?' he asked Zhi on impulse.

" 'Yes, of course, He already does,' replied his friend. Soon they were studying the Bible together. Chong became a new man and started sending money home to his parents instead of spending it on cigarettes and beer.

" 'If God can make a change like that in my son,' Chong's father told Chong the next time he was home on shore leave, 'then we want to believe in God too.' His father and mother soon became Christians."

On another occasion, Zhi decided to go fishing while the ship was in port. "Nobody ever catches fish in this port," yelled his fellow sailors from the ship when they saw him with his fishing pole. "If you catch even one fish, I'll go to church with you," one man said, laughing.

Zhi smiled, threw his line into the water, and prayed, "Lord, help me catch at least one fish so that guy will have to go to church with me." No sooner had he prayed than his line jerked, and he pulled out a sizable fish! Then he caught two more. The other sailor not only went to church with Zhi but started studying the Bible with him too.

Once Zhi's ship sheltered in a Philippine port because of a typhoon. In the dark of night, thieves boarded the ship with knives and guns, robbing the sailors on board.

"Give me your money!" One thief spoke in English to Zhi.

"I will not only give you my money, but I will also give you my most precious possession. It will be your greatest treasure," Zhi said as he held up his Mandarin-English Bible.

"Are you a Christian?" asked the startled thief.

"Yes," said Zhi. The thief took the Bible but only half of the money.

Some months later, while on shore leave in the same port, Zhi went into a restaurant for supper. While he was eating, the waitress brought him two more dishes of food. Surprised, Zhi protested, "I didn't order these."

"That man ordered them for you," the waitress said as she pointed to a man sitting near the window. Zhi looked over at the smiling man, whom he immediately recognized as the thief who had taken his Bible several months before. The man stood up and walked over to where Zhi was seated.

"Good to see you again." He was obviously eager to start a conversation. "I want to tell you about that money I stole from you," he began. "I took it that very day and gave it to an orphanage that needed it. Do you have time to come visit the orphanage?" he asked.

"Yes, that would be great," replied Zhi. Together they walked several blocks to the orphanage, where a priest confirmed the gift of money and gave them a tour of the children's home.

"I always wanted to help an orphanage," wrote Zhi to AWR. "This is the way the Lord helped me do it."

Some months later, a letter came from Zhi, whom we affectionately called our high seas missionary. He reported, "We have eight new sailors on our ship, all Vietnamese. Please send me some spiritual material I can give to them."

Our sailing missionary was still busy doing God's work.

Nineteen

Island Farewell

"There's a Japanese gentleman here to see you. He says he talked with you by telephone about . . . buying the station?" Sharon Guth, my secretary, turned her matter-of-fact statement into a question.

"Oh yes, please ask him to come in," I said, then whispered, "I'll tell you all about it after he leaves."

Mr. Takayama had the look of a typical prosperous executive. I was amused but also a little disturbed by his suggestion that he was interested in buying our radio station. I felt somewhat uneasy as we made ourselves comfortable around the big rectangular table in our Japanese Room. (We decorated each room of the station with artwork from one of the countries to which we broadcast, and I was glad at that moment that this room had a large mural of cherry blossoms on silk and another picture with a Japanese motif.)

"Our corporation has purchased three hundred acres of land surrounding your radio station," he began confidently. "We are planning to build four large hotels, hundreds of condominiums, an eighteen-hole golf course, a water park, and a shopping center." His words rolled out with lightning speed. I gripped the arms of my chair to control my panic.

"As part of these plans, we would like to offer you some land closer

Island Farewell

to the highway. Your old building here would become our clubhouse for the golf course!" His company obviously planned thoroughly. He leaned back to see whether I would accept his gracious offer.

"In principle, I have no objection to the plan at this time," I said. I was feeling my way as I answered slowly. "However, you need to know that I do not personally own the station, and I do not have the final say. I believe we will need to schedule some more meetings to discuss your offer."

Thus began several months of negotiations that would keep us in turmoil. We had difficulty comprehending why a move would be necessary, but at the same time, the company was offering a completely new physical plant and many additional dollars for our endowment fund to help us with long-term operational costs. We also imagined that our station might have difficulty operating in the middle of a golf course if we refused to move. We prayed daily for the Lord's help with this new challenge.

The AWR board chair, Ken Mittleider, came to lead our discussions with the corporation. Such a move, he cautioned, would be very costly and would take a couple of years to accomplish. It would have to be done totally at the corporation's expense, without any loss of airtime and with considerable compensation for the inconvenience caused by the disruption of station operations. It was difficult to concentrate on our work while such upheaval was in the offing.

In the end, however, the dilemma was resolved for us by a financial debt crisis in Japan. Mr. Takayama's company fell into financial difficulty and had to abandon its development project on Guam.

With all the challenges we faced on the island, we were always encouraged by the support from those on the US mainland. Every day checks, large and small, came to support the radio ministry. More than money, the warm wishes and assurance of our supporters' prayers buoyed our spirits.

"The Lord has blessed us, and we want to pass the blessing on: here is a check for $250," wrote one retired couple.

Another woman wrote, "I'm interested in doing something in my husband's memory."

And yet another person declared, "I am 87 years old today, so I am sending you a birthday gift to celebrate!"

"At long last, our home has sold, and we have collected the payoff.

A Japanese developer cited the AWR station on Guam as a prime property for commercial development. The photo shows the southern half of the station complex. Four more towers to the right of the building support three more antennas.

Accordingly, we are sending $10,000 to AWR," wrote a middle-aged couple.

A single woman wrote, "I saved a little from my living expenses, and I would be glad if this could be used for the radio ministry." She included a check for $500.

One man sent a donation and added this note: "I don't know how often I can send a gift. I'll send what I can. I've always prayed for your work, and I am thrilled with the results you are getting."

As the manager of Guam's AWR station, one of my annual chores was preparing a budget for the coming year. In preparing the budget for 1991, it appeared we would be $90,000 short of the funds needed. As I pondered and prayed about what to do, some incredible news arrived from church headquarters in Washington: a donor pledged a $1.3 million gift to AWR! Neal Wilson, the General Conference president, had been casting a vision to major donors about how they could ensure that AWR broadcasts reached out to the world in years to come. The endowment fund would benefit from this latest donation and would be greatly bolstered. At 1991's rate of 10 percent interest per year, income from the fund would be just over $100,000 per year for AWR's operation!

A dear church family shared the reason for their generous gift: they

Island Farewell

had decided the money from matured stocks in their company should go for the church's outreach in Asia. William L. Pascoe, AWR's new treasurer in Guam, arrived in early 1986. A retired treasurer who served in several parts of church administration around the world, William and his wife, Mona, were the newest additions to the AWR team. He was keeping close tabs on AWR's funding, and he told us that church headquarters had a goal of $10 million for the endowment fund.

This latest donation increased our endowment to $4,483,000, providing a major part of our annual budgeted income. It would be used solely for keeping our transmitters running for years to come. Our electrical costs were ten cents per kilowatt hour, and with electricity on the island generated by diesel generators, electricity was a major expense in our budget. Of course, interest rates were bound to fluctuate, but the added income from the endowment would always help to fill budget gaps, whatever the current interest rate.

With such support, we were given the courage to think and plan on a larger scale. There were so many more people in the world who needed to hear the good news. We carried a constant burden for vast areas that we could not reach yet. One such country was Russia, the world's largest landmass. Russia sprawled over Europe and Asia, and much of its territory was in Guam's station coverage area.

In late 1991, I was asked to visit Russia with AWR's new director, Walter Scragg, to see whether we could assist in developing a new media center in the city of Tula; it would be Russia's first private media center. Russian radio programs would be made available to many of the nation's eleven time zones.

Peter Kulakov, the media center director in Tula, Russia, was happy to meet two fellow broadcasters who were anxious to see what had been accomplished. We found workers climbing all over the shell of a sizable building. We advised Peter on how to best situate the radio studios and asked how soon programs in Russian would be available for broadcast. "As soon as our studio is operational, we will send you programs," he promised.

On March 31, 1992, AWR-Asia began broadcasts to Russia. Soon listener letters arrived from all over that country—from Vladivostok in Siberia on the Pacific Ocean to the Baltic republics in the west. The letters reported a strong signal.

"I want to know more about the Adventist Church," wrote Vasily from central Siberia. "Do you follow both the Old and New Testaments? Please help me find the road to truth."

In another letter from the same region, Aleksey wrote, "Thank you very much for your programs that help me understand more about our Lord Jesus."

"I have always dreamed of having a Bible. Can you send me one?" wrote Dimitry in Moscow.

Another listener in Moscow wrote, "I work as a locksmith. I like listening to your programs in English. Thanks to them, I can learn more about our Lord. For a long time, I have dreamed about having my own Holy Bible. Would you send me one and some other spiritual literature?"

It was thrilling to see responses coming in from around the world and to see how AWR-Asia had grown since the first transmitter went on the air for eight hours a day on March 6, 1987, and broadcast in fourteen languages. By 1992, AWR reported fifty thousand pieces of mail had been received at the Guam station from listeners.

Thanks to the liberal support from church members, the Guam station had proven radio's ability not only to reach into the world's twenty-five largest megacities, such as Tokyo, Bombay (now Mumbai), Seoul, and Beijing, but also to pierce the rural parts of Asia—the rice paddies, farms, and mountaintops where individuals in isolation found the AWR signal. That type of coverage would be needed in other parts of the world.

On the long trip to Russia, Walter and I strategized about the future of AWR. As the first full-time director, he was eager to see how the goal of reaching the whole world could be achieved, given limited church resources.

When I returned to Guam, I shared the gist of our talks with Andrea. "No doubt there will be changes in our AWR operations, maybe even some relocation of staff," I said.

"Oh, it would be very hard to leave Guam," she sighed. Indeed, we had greatly enjoyed life on the tropical island.

Just a few days after those comments, I received a call from Walter. He asked if we would be willing to return to Europe, where he felt we could better serve as program and public relations directors for the AWR worldwide system. With new excitement about what we might be able to accomplish in a wider role, it wasn't long before we found ourselves packing boxes again for a return to the other side of the globe.

Twenty

Europe Landing

"You say it has nice big windows? And it's only a ten-minute walk to the office?" Andrea asked after a steady stream of questions. She could hardly believe I found such a nice apartment after everything we had heard about the difficulties newcomers encounter when looking for a place to live in crowded Germany.

"In the worst-case scenario, you might even have to purchase and install your own kitchen—sink, cupboards, and all," Walter Scragg had warned us. But just like Andrea, he was pleasantly surprised when Claudius Dedio, our new AWR colleague, reported that he found a furnished apartment for us, conveniently located on *Heidelberger Landstrasse* (one of the main roads) in Darmstadt, Germany. It was on a streetcar line to downtown Darmstadt and only around sixteen miles (twenty-five kilometers) from the large central city of Frankfurt am Main and its large international airport. It was also not far from my old stomping grounds when I was stationed as an army soldier, just east of Frankfurt in the town of Hanau on the river Main.

Andrea was further amazed when, on our first day in Germany, we climbed the stairs and entered the nicely appointed four-room apartment. She went from room to room, touching every counter, chair, and cupboard.

"I think it will be good for us to have an apartment; it will give us more time for our work at AWR," she added as she started unpacking our clothes and placing them neatly in the bedroom chest of drawers. I was thankful for a reprieve from yard work because it looked like our travel schedule in this new job would have us out of town much of the time.

We were immediately drawn to our landlady, Frau Scharf, who quickly became a dear friend. She was a widow and welcomed us as if we were family and then proceeded to spoil us as if we were her very own kin. She developed a habit of cooking a lovely fruit torte for us whenever we returned from long trips. She often invited us to join her and her friends for supper on her back terrace; the terrace overlooked a private garden that displayed a wide variety of flowering plants and fruit trees. In the middle of the garden was a small fountain that gurgled down into a little pond filled with water lilies and goldfish.

AWR had only recently made the decision to move its European headquarters to Darmstadt to take advantage of its central European location and its convenient travel and communication amenities. Greg Hodgson was the regional director for Europe, Claudius was the chief engineer, and Pino Cirillo was his assistant engineer. Our assignment, which was no easy task, was to work with this European team and, at the same time, for the worldwide AWR system. None of us were sure how this arrangement would work, but we were happy to be together as a team, which made us willing to try anything.

It took us some time to grasp everything that had happened to AWR in Europe in recent years. The continent was in the turmoil of change, caused mostly by the collapse of Communism in Eastern Europe. East Germany and West Germany had reunited, and numerous countries of the former Soviet Bloc had either achieved independence or were working toward it.

AWR suddenly had opportunities to begin broadcasting in former Communist countries. The Seventh-day Adventist Church had been foremost in advancing its activities as the doors of freedom opened. It was the first Protestant church to establish a theological seminary in Russia, the first to build and open a printing house, and the first to go nationwide with radio and television programs. These efforts positioned the church well for the opportunity that AWR would soon have for shortwave broadcasts on former Radio Moscow transmitters.

Europe Landing

From left, Novosibirsk radio manager Vladimir Myasnikov signs the agreement with AWR to rent antennas for AWR's use. Looking on are Yuri Vedernikov, chief engineer; Peter Kulakoff, director of the Russian media center; Walter Scragg, AWR director; and Kenneth Mittleider, AWR board chair, 1991.

"Almost unbelievable" was how Walter described an offer from broadcast officials in Russia. In response to inquiries about the possible lease of airtime on former Radio Moscow transmitters in Siberia, AWR was offered the opportunity to lease a transmitter especially aimed at southern Asia.

A contract between the Voice of Hope Media Center in Tula, Russia, and the cooperative managing the powerful shortwave station in Novosibirsk, Siberia, would take AWR programming to the airwaves twenty-three hours every day. The very propaganda facilities that had jammed AWR broadcasts on Radio Trans-Europe in Portugal for so many years would now be broadcasting AWR programs!

"It was bitingly cold in Siberia," Walter said about the inauguration of the broadcasts. "It was forty below zero, centigrade and Fahrenheit [forty below is the one place where the two temperature scales read the same], but we were warm inside because of the momentous occasion." He described the emotional experience as AWR became the first Western broadcaster to go on air using the former Communist propaganda stations.

A local woman in the city where the ceremony took place stood up during the church service to tell how she prayed for fifty years that those mighty transmitters she could see in the distance would one day be used by the Lord for His purposes. There were very few dry eyes as she gave her testimony.

"We live in a day of miracles," said Kenneth Mittleider, AWR board chair, speaking about the Russian broadcasts in 1992. "Two years ago such a possibility would have been laughed to scorn, yet today it is a reality," he added.[1]

With the advent of programming from Russia, the end of an era came for AWR at the Radio Trans-Europe site in Portugal. On Sunday, June 28, 1992, AWR broadcast its final programs from Portugal. For twenty years, that station had been our major voice for a large part of the world. But because the airtime costs had climbed so high, programming decreased to only seven and a half hours per week. The Siberian stations would now replace it as the major voice of AWR.

While we were rejoicing over the new developments in Russia, stories of success continued to come in from other parts of the world in response to our programs—and not just from individuals and families but whole groups of people who warmed to the Adventist message with the broadcasts from Guam and Russia.

From Indochina, pastors of three churches wrote to say they were using material from the AWR broadcasts as sermons in their own churches, and one group was even using the AWR broadcast on Wednesday evenings as their midweek prayer meeting.

The coordinator for an independent gospel ministry in Sri Lanka wrote, "We have ten branch churches, and we extend expertise and advice to six emerging churches. We have a number of home cells and other enterprises to take the love and redeeming power of our Lord to our neighbors. We also do a lot of counseling. In spite of civil strife here, people are drawing closer to our Lord. We would like to get transcripts of your broadcasts."

In Africa, AWR was continuing its purchase of airtime on Radio Africa No. 1 in Gabon. As the most powerful station on the big continent, it provided an excellent signal into West and Central Africa. Seven hours of programs per week were not much, but the results were heartwarming.

The president of a church in Nigeria wrote, "We are members of a Bible-believing and practicing church. Having regularly listened to your broadcast and having critically examined your doctrinal expositions, we have discovered that we have identical visions and beliefs. Consequently, we are requesting affiliation with your ministry."

Members of another church in Nigeria said, "We wish to let you

Europe Landing

know that we are avid listeners to AWR. We listen to your evening programs and take them as our evening studies. Long live AWR!"

A letter written on behalf of several people from a village in Benin said: "We have received the whole good news in its purity." The group was already active in witnessing by organizing a musical group of guitarists. They began an AWR ministry in their town of Azovè. They presented public concerts and gave short sermons to those who attended.

In another village in Benin, an Adventist man was selling religious books house to house, searching for people who had graduated from the AWR Bible course to see whether they cared to purchase any religious literature.

"Yes, of course," said a man who opened the first door the colporteur came to. "We are Seventh-day Adventists! Come, let me show you something."

Together they walked to a small church building, where the man pointed to the sign over the door, which read "Adventist World Radio Church." He turned the sign over; there was the name of another denomination. Nearly the whole church of seventy members had voted to become Seventh-day Adventists.

Eight church members in Notsé, Togo, who were AWR listeners, joined workers from the Adventist dental clinic in the town of Glei to form another congregation. The new church was located roughly ten miles (seventeen kilometers) from Lomé, the country's capital.

Meanwhile, the search was on for a site where we could build our own AWR-Africa station, beginning with a possibility in Liberia, but political unrest in that country ruled it out as a safe location. Two other options seemed feasible: Namibia in southern Africa or the island nation of São Tomé and Príncipe in the Atlantic Ocean. I joined Walter on an exploratory trip to the latter in the Gulf of Guinea. Previously a Portuguese territory, the islands were ideally poised to send a strong radio signal to most of western Africa.

After a visit with the country's president, we trudged through the tropical jungle to visit a couple of the suggested building sites. As we plodded along the jungle paths, we passed the small homes of residents who watched us from their front doorsteps. Fortunately, before leaving Germany, I bought a bag of balloons that I now filled with air and presented to the children along the way. They were a big hit and brought smiles to both parents and children. After a couple of days there, we returned to Europe to write a report on our trip.

Another exciting AWR project was taking place on another island, far from São Tomé. Church leaders in the Middle East decided to install a media center on the island of Cyprus where Arabic, Farsi, and Turkish programs could be prepared for broadcast on AWR.

Neal Wilson, the former president of the world church, now retired, had worked for some years in the Middle East, and a fund drive was established in his honor to benefit the new project. The goal for the project was set at $25,000, but more than $35,000 was donated, and the new center officially opened in 1992. Within a short time, AWR was able to broadcast up to eight hours a day of Arabic programs to the Middle East, with Bert Smit directing the new Adventist Media Centre–Middle East.

Bert was desperate for program materials for the many hours of new programs in Arabic. He heard rumors that some old program tapes existed, produced some years before the broadcasts on Radio Trans-Europe. They had disappeared during the civil war years in Lebanon.

Attempts to find the tapes were fruitless until, while visiting Beirut, Lebanon, in early 1993, Bert and his colleague Amir Ghali were poking around in an abandoned church office, which had been extensively damaged by mortars during the war. They discovered the lost treasure in an old cabinet in the corner of the building. Providentially, dozens of tapes in three languages were there, just waiting to be discovered.

"There is a whole series on health, mostly still relevant today," said Bert. "The classical Arabic is of very good quality, and with minor editing, we can use all the tapes. It is a wonderful find, and we praise God for it."

Back in Europe, we heard of a young man in the Polish military who had an incredible experience with AWR. He was training as a paratrooper. His workweek consisted of repeated parachute jumps.

"One day we were up in the air for one of our regular practice jumps," he wrote.

> As I jumped, something happened that had never happened before. The guy right behind me was not paying attention and jumped almost immediately after I did. As our parachutes opened with the whip of the wind, they became incredibly entangled. We

both were fighting desperately to untangle those parachutes while falling faster and faster toward the ground.

All the time, one question was racing through my mind: Is this it, God; is this the end for me? What will happen to me when I die, God? What will happen?

Finally, we don't know how, we were able to untangle ourselves enough to jettison the entangled chutes. We got rid of that extra baggage just in time to open our emergency chutes. We landed on the ground with a thud. But the question in my mind persisted: What will happen when I die?

He was incredibly shaken by the accident. That night, trying to forget the harrowing experience, he turned on the radio. The first program that he heard in Polish was the *Voice of Hope* on AWR. The topic was "What Happens When You Die?" He couldn't believe his ears. Of course, he signed up for the Bible course that was offered. He later became a member of an Adventist church in his city.

---

1. "Red Square Station to Broadcast Adventism," News, *North Pacific Union Gleaner*, May 18, 1992, 19.

Twenty-One

The Banner Years

The early 1990s turned out to be banner years for AWR. Weekly hours on the air topped one thousand, the number of transmitters in use expanded to sixteen, and nearly fifty studios were busy producing programs in forty languages.

"There's an amazing thing about all this," Walter Scragg said to us one day when he and his wife, Elizabeth—a much-appreciated member of the AWR team—were visiting us in Darmstadt. "Of all the major broadcasters, we probably have the smallest staff! We have become adept at doing much with few resources."

I had to admit it was true. Under Walter's leadership, we all developed a motto of "putting money into broadcast hours."

Programming, of course, was my full-time concern as program director for the worldwide network. My part-time responsibility for programming turned into a full-time job as AWR expanded and as needs around the world increased. I was also tasked with training and audience research. With Walter's encouragement, we were able to establish a program resource center at Newbold College, England, to provide materials to help producers create attractive programs. Ray Allen, a former student missionary for AWR in Portugal, was asked to lead out in that new office.

The Banner Years

Robert Folkenberg *(left)* and Garwin McNeilus *(right)* inaugurate the AWR-Latin America station at Cahuita, Costa Rica, in 1992. Sharing the moment are F. Martin Ytreberg, AWR treasurer *(second left)*, and Walter Scragg, AWR director *(second from right)*. In the background is the wife of a local government official and Raymond Lenz, station chief engineer.

On July 8, 1992, Robert Folkenberg, president of the world church, had the pleasure of presiding at the dedication and start of broadcasts from a new AWR shortwave station in Cahuita, Costa Rica. In addition to a station in Guatemala, started earlier, four more transmitters were now broadcasting from Costa Rica, thanks especially to the financial help of Marilee and Garwin McNeilus, a dedicated Adventist couple in the United States. David Gregory, station manager, said the new broadcasts could be heard as far south as Brazil and as far north as Canada.

Folkenberg said, "AWR is one of the most direct ways to turn cash into mission." His conviction about the need for radio to reach the world came some years earlier when he was stationed in Guatemala. He went on to cofound AWR's first Latin American station in Guatemala City in 1979 with the financial help of Willma and Olov Blomquist.

In September 1993, we published our first systemwide program schedule. We were now presenting ourselves as a worldwide entity. As such, we became known as one of the world's largest international broadcasters and a leading Christian voice on the airwaves. Our theme song, "Lift Up the Trumpet," was familiar around the world.

AWR operations soon were known by the regions where we broadcast. AWR-Europe came first when we started broadcasts from Portugal in 1971. AWR-Asia and AWR-Latin America began in the late 1970s under pioneers Adrian Peterson and Robert Folkenberg, respectively. Daniel Grisier led the development of AWR-Africa in the 1980s, and AWR-Russia was developed in the early 1990s under the leadership of Peter Kulakov.

In 1994, AWR leaders convened a planning commission to study how operations could be streamlined. To minimize the duplication of the efforts in its regional offices, the commission decided to centralize the administration in a single location, which was still to be determined. We had an exceptional team of talented leaders in the regional locations, and I appreciated and valued the contributions of each one.

"Take Greg Hodgson, for example," I said to Andrea one day as we were discussing our work. "His persistence in trying to get permission to build an AWR shortwave station in Italy is incredible." For the 1990 General Conference offering, church leaders had agreed to create a fund for building the station, and in 1995, the funds were still in an

Standing, Walter Scragg, Greg Hodgson, and Kenneth Mittleider join hands with the Radio Slovakia engineers to start the first broadcast of that station in 1994.

The Banner Years

account, awaiting the day when the new facility could be built. Greg continued urging the Italian government to pass legislation to permit such a station. When it became clear that his plan could not be realized, he began searching for an alternative. He found it in Slovakia.

Radio Slovakia came as a heaven-sent opportunity for AWR in 1994. The Communists had built one of the most effective international stations in the world in the city of Rimavská Sobota. It was known as Radio Prague during its propaganda days, but now, with the peaceful split of Czechoslovakia into the Czech Republic and the Slovak Republic, this remarkable facility became a prime target for use by AWR.

As soon as possible after the great political changes in Eastern Europe, Greg began probing officials in Prague and Bratislava about the potential for purchasing airtime on the Rimavská Sobota station. It had powerful 250-kilowatt transmitters connected to some of the world's largest and most effective antennas, known as 8 × 8 curtains. This gave the station a tremendous broadcast range, reaching into Africa, Asia, Europe, the Americas, and the Middle East.

Repeated requests to Radio Slovakia bore fruit in late 1993 when AWR was granted a license to broadcast over stations in the republic. AWR immediately contracted for the full-time use of two transmitters. On January 1, 1994, the first test transmissions were heard from the station. Regular broadcasts began from Rimavská Sobota on January 8, when AWR leaders joined state officials in Bratislava for the official opening ceremony.

The opening came none too soon. The Russian stations, which had bargain prices for airtime when they first became available, drastically increased their prices year after year and, by 1994, began pricing themselves beyond AWR's budget. This would also eventually become a problem in Slovakia when prices would double within two years.

Nevertheless, the Radio Slovakia station expanded our capabilities tremendously. We now had a signal that boomed into the Middle East like a local station.

"During the first three months of 1995, three hundred letters arrived at the Bible school from listeners in the Middle East," reported Bert Smit. "We had letters from every country in the region, and a considerable number came from countries where the church has no established work," he declared.

He reported that in one country, listeners formed a Voice of Hope

The first four AWR managers at the Utrecht General Conference session. *From left*, Allen Steele, Ron Myers, Mike Wiist, and Greg Hodgson.

Radio Club. "They listen to AWR together on a regular basis," he told us. "But in more restricted areas, new believers worship secretly around the radio."

In Baghdad, Iraq, a Seventh-day Adventist church welcomed many new members who started attending their services. Most of them first came to the church to get books that were promoted on the Arabic radio programs.

"I am a Muslim Asian employed in the United Arab Emirates," wrote one listener. "I have been listening to AWR for the last few days, and it is through this broadcast that Jesus Christ and the Holy Bible are introduced to me, and my soul is enlightened with this teaching. There is an inspirational and educational balance in your programs, thus attracting someone to be a regular listener. I would like to receive your Bible study, but such printed matter is prohibited here. So AWR is my main source of inspiration."

A listener in Egypt wrote, "To my best, my favorite, and my dearest station, AWR—the *Voice of Hope*: Your station enlightens the way for the young people and comforts them."

From Iraq, a young listener wrote, "I plead with you to take my hand and guide me, teach me, and get me out of my perplexity."

AWR built a broadcast center at the 1995 General Conference Session in Utrecht, Netherlands, to accommodate fifty broadcasters who came to cover the event. Andrea Steele is at far left. Greg Hodgson sits on the front row with a sprained ankle.

"This is my fifth letter to my favorite station," a listener from a North African country wrote in Arabic. "Thanks to you, I now believe in Jesus Christ and believe He is the Son of God. But I still need some clarification about the relationship between the Father and the Son."

Another young man in North Africa told of his experience:

> I would hold my radio close to my ear with the volume turned way down so no one else could hear. The program was called the *Voice of Hope* and came over Adventist World Radio.
>
> Just being a Christian was risky enough without going to a faraway town where people would watch my every move. I was baptized by an evangelical pastor in 1983. But the producers of the AWR program remembered me, and one day to my complete surprise, the *Voice of Hope* speaker visited me.
>
> About this time, persecution stepped up, and our little group of Christians disbanded. I was also beginning to understand what was special about Seventh-day Adventists. I had accepted the Bible as God's inspired word, and I saw the importance of the seventh day, but I was impressed with Adventist health principles and lifestyle. Some of the evangelicals would smoke and drink, and they ate pork.
>
> I found logic and what I call "spiritual reason" in what Adventists taught. Someone sent me a book, *The Great Controversy*. For

the first time, I read the history of Christianity, and that made me take the Bible even more seriously. This was an extraordinary experience.

Thankfully, our withdrawal from the shortwave stations in Russia didn't decrease our listenership. Our media center in Tula was able to obtain program time on national radio networks in all the countries of the former Soviet Union. Most homes there had been wired for radio (somewhat like a cable television system), creating one of the world's largest radio audiences.

AWR's *Voice of Hope* program became the most popular religious radio program in Russia. According to a national audience research project, we had four million listeners each week. The listener response was so heavy that our media center had difficulty in processing all the mail. And it was not only our media center but the post office as well.

"You have nearly four thousand letters here," the postmaster reported by telephone one day. "Would you please come and get them," he pleaded, "so we can sort the rest of the mail?"

In a short time, the media center could point to many new churches around Russia that had their beginning from *Voice of Hope* broadcasts. In the city of Tula itself, the radio broadcasts brought in a large part of the membership of the new Central Seventh-day Adventist Church.

The year 1995 was another pivotal year in AWR history. The church's General Conference meetings would be held in Utrecht, Netherlands. These meetings often determine major changes in the Seventh-day Adventist Church, and many leadership changes take place. AWR would be no exception at the fifty-sixth General Conference session. Walter Scragg, now holding the title of AWR president, privately informed us that he planned to retire. During his four years as our leader, we witnessed incredible growth in the reach and results of AWR's ministry.

To celebrate AWR's contribution to the growth of the church, we decided to create a special exhibit and broadcast worldwide reports on the events at the Utrecht convocation. I was asked to lead in the planning of a broadcast center where programs would be produced in twenty languages.

To accommodate the fifty broadcasters, we constructed our own broadcast center in the convention hall. It was an impressive structure, located at the crossroads of session activities in the convention center. It housed seven recording studios, a master control room for sending out radio programs to the world, a local radio station, and offices. These were all clustered around a large work area that contained computer editing desks and recording edit stations. The whole center had windows strategically located to provide viewing from outside, where streams of people passed by, constantly observing our work in progress.

We positioned our rented satellite uplink dish just outside the convention hall. Day and night, programs went up to a satellite and from there were beamed to the transmitters in Europe, Africa, Asia, and the Middle East. Programs for the Americas and Asia were sent through a combination telephone-satellite system to our stations in Costa Rica and Guam.

The session broadcasts were a huge success. Many stories were later reported of people who were attracted to the Adventist message because of these special broadcasts. While we were there, three young Muslim employees at the Royal Dutch Jaarbeurs Exhibition and Convention Center, where the session was held, signed up for Bible studies at the AWR exhibit. It was a demonstration of how media could be used to witness to the world with a major church event as its focus—a method later adopted by Adventist television networks.

Gordon Retzer, AWR president, 1996–1997.

These were exciting days, working alongside fellow broadcasters from around the world for nearly two weeks. A special treat at the session was being with my three fellow managers of AWR-Europe: Ron Myers, who replaced me, working at Radio Trans-Europe in Portugal until 1981; Michael Wiist, who served three years until 1985; and the current manager, Greg Hodgson, who followed Wiist.

The General Conference session came to an end, but several decisions made at the session would guide our work until the next General Conference in five years: Walter Scragg tendered his resignation, and Gordon Retzer, manager of the Guam station, was elected the new president of AWR.

Another decision would affect Andrea and me more profoundly. In Germany, the deutsche mark had reached new highs against the US dollar, and the cost of operating in Germany was becoming prohibitive. As a result, AWR decided to move the system offices. It was decided that Andrea and I would relocate to a new location—Britain.

Twenty-Two

A British Sojourn

Our flight from Frankfurt to England was the shortest household move we ever experienced in our years with AWR. A quick hop of just over an hour landed us in our new home country. Still ahead was the challenge of finding office space and a place to live. We already had a link to Newbold College located in Bracknell, just west of London, where Ray Allen was still creating program ideas for AWR producers at our AWR Program Resource Center—a small radio studio on campus. But the college did not have any extra space to offer for our offices.

The search for a home and office began once we were in the country. While we searched, we temporarily rented an apartment in St. Albans, north of London. Our search was interrupted by a trip to church headquarters in the United States in the fall of 1995. While there, we welcomed the new AWR president and joined the board of directors at their annual meeting.

We were only a couple of days into our round of meetings when an urgent message came from England. A fire had broken out in the warehouse where the moving company kept our storage container! According to the police report, the entire warehouse was consumed by the fire, which was probably caused by a fault in the electrical wiring of the building. The building that burned down also housed cars and furniture owned by other families.

"Oh no," Andrea and I both gasped. "All of our office files were in that container!" We staggered through several days of shock, every minute trying to remember what actually had been shipped to England in that container, which was the first of five. Most of our clothes were in it, but no worry, we could do with new wardrobes. But many of the historical and office business files, books, and materials were now gone forever.

It was then that I realized why the Lord laid a strong conviction on me to write *Loud Let It Ring!*—a book about the first twenty-five years of AWR—before we left the continent. I'd spent many midnight hours frantically working on the manuscript, and now I knew it was God who was urging me to get the book completed before we moved to Britain. (That little book, my editor told me, was the first manuscript that any author had sent to him by internet.) It recorded the important history of AWR and would now be the primary reference for facts related to that incredible early history. God wanted that story to be recorded, and He honored me by permitting me to tell it.

Our meetings at the church's headquarters turned out to be remarkable. It soon became obvious to us how important AWR had become for the advancement of God's work on Earth. Our radio ministry was increasing church growth around the world, yet we were forced to find ways to cut our budget for 1996—our budget requests were $700,000 more than our projected income. But with the help of Richard Green, the new AWR treasurer, we were able to present a balanced budget.

Gordon Retzer, the new AWR president, pledged to operate AWR on as economical a basis as possible, even while we added more languages to our program schedule and upgraded our facilities using new technologies. He asked the board to approve a goal to fund a total of one hundred languages by 2001. "To operate economically," he added, "we will concentrate on keeping overhead expenses lean so that we can fund the expanded broadcast schedule." He focused on a concept of centralized administration and fewer persons located at radio stations.

I was excited to hear Retzer commit AWR to the use of new technologies. "We are interested in utilizing any new technology that will help AWR accomplish its mission," he said. As I recalled my final academic project at Andrews University—my dissertation on the effective use of satellite by the church—I thought, *It would be a thrill to witness my theory being put into action.*

Retzer was also able to report the arrival of the third transmitter on Guam for AWR-Asia. "It's on the air, tested, and already bringing results since its installation in August 1994," he announced. "The new transmitter allows the addition of three more languages and enables the station to carry 33 percent more prime-time broadcasts to the countries of Asia."

The church administration in Southeast Asia was especially happy to finally have programs for the country of Vietnam. Attempts to obtain programming in Vietnamese culminated when a young pastor in California committed to producing programs by setting up a recording studio in his home garage. Isaiah Duong, the pastor of the Loma Linda, California, Vietnamese Church, was already excitedly reporting results from listeners. He said there were sixty million people who spoke Vietnamese, most of whom were Buddhists, Confucians, and Taoists.

"In the last several days, I have met the Lord through your program," wrote a listener in Vietnam, who was a Catholic priest. "I am sure many families who have lost peace and happiness will find them when they listen to this program. I myself have experienced this. Please send me your material so I can lead the members of my parish back to Jesus Christ."

Another letter was from the leader of a group in a refugee camp in a country neighboring Vietnam. He reported that the camp would soon be closed, and the Vietnamese inmates would be repatriated to their homeland. No clergy was allowed to visit the camp, and food and other supplies were reduced to a bare minimum. The man explained his situation:

> Our church is the first and only church in the camp. We prayed and prayed to be guided by God, and my family and one hundred other families in the church decided we would return to Vietnam when the time came. While we were waiting, God's gift came. We received a Bible, books, and magazines from your *Peace and Happiness* radio program heard on AWR. No words can express our thanks, first to our Almighty God and then to every brother and sister on the program. You have given us new strength and reassured our faith in God.

Every day, we await the AWR nightly worship service. The radio speaker is our teacher and our friend. We often wonder what he will give us each night. The young people prefer sermons on how to have a happy marriage, the older people like the subject of how to have a happy family. Children love Bible stories. Your broadcast is the spiritual food that we cannot miss. It is the food that we must have in our lives, especially the lives of our people in refugee camps.

Our church does not have a pastor, so we regard the radio pastor as our unofficial teacher. We witness and study the Bible together or in groups. We will go back to Vietnam with only a small bag on our shoulders and nothing more. However, everyone is hopeful and in good spirits because in that bag will be a fortune: a Bible and some books about God. What else do we need anyway?

Programs in Urdu, another language new to AWR, also took to the air in the last half of 1994. This major language in Pakistan and India was also bringing results. "I like your program, *Voice of Hope*, very much," wrote a Pakistani listener in Saudi Arabia. "I am so encouraged and inspired. Religious songs touch me very much. I am a singer myself. When I come to Pakistan, I will sing for AWR free of cost. I am a Muslim, but in my heart, I am a Christian. I have accepted Christ as my Savior."

A tailor in Nepal began the habit of listening to AWR daily as he worked with his hands and sewing machine. He became a faithful follower of the messages he heard every day. He decided to rename his shop "The Jesus Tailor Shop." Soon after, an old friend came to visit, and a lively discussion ensued.

"What does that mean, 'The Jesus Tailor Shop'? What is Jesus?" he asked. With eyes beaming, the tailor told his friend about the wonderful news he had learned on the radio: the news that Jesus came to Earth, lived, died, and was resurrected, and because of this, the tailor did not have to worry about the future. So he put Jesus' name on his shop's sign.

His friend was interested, so they began to study the Bible together. One day the friend said, "I am nearly convinced, but I would like to see prayer really working." He posed a test to the tailor. "You complain about that cow you have out back that doesn't give milk. If you pray to Jesus and that cow gives milk, I will be convinced!"

The tailor decided to try. After all, he believed in Jesus' power to save him, so why couldn't He make the cow give milk? Still, when the man went to the cowshed and began to pray, there was a tremble in his voice. Would God think this a silly request? After praying, he went back to his shop to work.

A little later, he was impressed to go to the cowshed again. He took a pail, pulled up a stool, and began to milk—and the milk came in a steady stream! The tailor ran from the shed to fetch his friend, who stood and watched, eyes round with wonder, as the smiling, laughing tailor milked the cow—the Jesus cow! Both men became true followers of Christ.

Back in the Americas, AWR-Latin America continued to broadcast to Central American countries. From Guatemala came the story of Maria. Maria was angry. She was violent; she made everyone in her family afraid and unhappy. She even beat her husband! In her town, all the neighbors did everything they could to avoid her when they saw her coming.

Then one day, twenty-five-year-old Maria heard the story of Jesus on AWR and heard how He could give her a new life. After some weeks of listening to the programs, she stopped hitting her husband. Then her neighbors noticed that she was kinder, friendlier, and more accepting. The change was so complete that they began to seek her counsel.

"I promised God," she said, "that I would never beat my husband again. The *Voice of Hope* programs have given me hope. I don't need to be violent or afraid ever again."

For AWR, a coveted target in the region was Cuba. Forty percent of the mail to AWR was from the island—the largest country in the Caribbean with a population of eight million people. Young people were in the majority; it was estimated that nearly one-fourth of the population was less than fifteen years old.

"We can't even afford to send you any donations to indicate our support for your broadcasts which we enjoy so much," wrote a listener. "This really bothers us because your station brought us tremendous blessing through its message of hope and its informative programs on the present state of our mission here on this earth and the signs of the times."

Ricardo, another listener, a young man in his twenties, wrote:

> I hope you will tell many people about how I came to serve Jesus as a result of AWR's programs. When I began medical school, I didn't know anything about religion. One of my classmates asked me to listen to a radio program with him. It was that program, and a couple of others, that brought me to Christ.
>
> After my classmate and I listened to these programs, I started looking for a church where I could worship. I went to one and then another, but neither of them taught what I learned from the *Voice of Hope* radio program. Finally, I found an Adventist church and realized this was where God wanted me to be.
>
> Now, five of my classmates from medical school are Adventists. They are all doctors. Even the guy who ridiculed us for our interest in religion now studies the Bible. Every day I pray for AWR's staff and your other listeners. You are doing a wonderful work for Jesus.

Twenty-Three

At Home in England

Our search for an office in England was rewarded when we discovered a two-story house for sale across the street from Newbold College. It had five bedrooms that would serve well as offices and other large rooms that could be turned into production studios or equipment storage areas. There was also a parking area in front, and the location was ideal for the employment of college students as assistants in our public relations, programming, and European regional headquarters office.

With our working situation organized, Andrea and I began looking for a house to call home. We discovered an attractive red-brick semidetached home that was available just a couple of blocks from the office. (The house was termed *semidetached* because our outer garage wall served as a common wall for both our neighbor and us.) For the first time, we lived close enough to our workplace to be able to walk to work.

We were now the newest residents in the village of Binfield, in the borough of Bracknell Forest, in the Royal County of Berkshire. Fortunately, we were also within an hour's drive of London's Heathrow Airport. This would be important in our work for AWR because of the frequent travel we would need to make to the far-flung operations around the world.

Binfield, which is just west of Windsor, is famous as the home of the poet Alexander Pope. His poem "Windsor-Forest" hints at the importance of the royal hunting grounds that stretched from Windsor Castle to Binfield. (They were important to King Henry VIII and his second wife, Anne Boleyn, whose daughter became Queen Elizabeth I.) A couple of blocks north of Newbold College was the Stag and Hounds Pub, which claimed to be a favorite feasting place for Henry VIII's entourage after their fox hunts in the forest.

The city of Bracknell, next to the village of Binfield, was one of the "new towns" created after the Second World War to house families who were bombed out of their homes in London. During the Second World War's famous Blitz of London, thousands of misplaced Londoners were encouraged to move outside the city for safety and to recover from the trauma of war. Bracknell then became a commercial center, and for us, it was our nearest shopping center.

Our few years in this historic location were personally rewarding, mostly for the many new friendships we developed with faculty members from the college but also for our association with students who came to study from around the world. One of our most memorable occasions was a Christmas meal we prepared for some students from Korea and Japan. They were far from home and in a place where the holiday was very important, unlike most places in Asia. They were studying English at Newbold, and our conversations during the meal and afterward were interesting and quite comical at times. Other students of different nationalities, including Americans, were often guests in our home.

To expand our space for entertaining, we added what in England is called a conservatory to the rear of our house, attached to the kitchen. It was basically a glassed-in room with views of our back garden, and it became an ideal venue for entertaining, not only for college students but for many other guests who visited, including fellow AWR staff members.

In the spring of 1997, our president, Gordon Retzer, was enticed away from AWR to become president of the church's Florida Conference in America's Southeast. Don Jacobsen, a former professor of mine at Andrews University, was chosen as our new leader. In my studies at the theological seminary, I chose his class on church administration as part of my academic program.

At about the same time, Robert Folkenberg, president of the world church, announced a plan to connect the church's growing mission to the world in a new way to coordinate its ministries and services around the world. "In a world of great diversity, our challenge is to use modern methods to share our message," he announced. With these words, he declared the church would install a global satellite program distribution system for radio and television. He set a goal of 1999 for full implementation of the satellite network.

It was a significant shift in the way the church would relate to its mission of reaching "every nation, and kindred, and tongue, and people" in the world (Revelation 14:6). Diversified approaches would be needed to fulfill Scripture's mandate. For AWR, this method of sharing program material with radio stations was quickly becoming a convenient way to provide instant information and programs to our radio stations. The days of reel-to-reel tapes and cassette recordings of programs were about to end.

Jacobsen also took up the leadership reins at a time when AWR needed to consider new ways to make significant changes in the nature of its broadcast operations. It was the start of a revolution in numerous parts of the world in regard to religious radio broadcasting; more governments were issuing licenses for local radio stations. In several countries where governments previously controlled all broadcasting, local AM and FM private stations were now permitted. It was happening in France, Italy, Scandinavian countries, Brazil, and Bolivia, in addition to the United States, where such freedom was already long established.

Don Jacobsen, AWR president, 1998–2001.

To take advantage of these advances by the world church, Don asked me to be AWR's vice president for strategic planning. It was a new role that would consume all of my imagination and energy. Andrea would continue as the public relations director for the network, which meant there would probably be more divergences in our paths.

It wasn't long before I was assigned the job of visiting Latin American countries to encourage a cooperative effort among the Spanish-speaking radio stations that were popping up from Puerto Rico to Chile. AWR's plan was to establish a network using satellite to distribute programs to existing and future local radio stations. It would lighten the financial burdens for the sponsors of those stations, which, in many cases, were local conferences or local churches.

But the challenge was where to obtain the programs that the local stations could use. My strategy was to encourage each station to develop a one-hour Spanish segment that could be shared with all the stations around the Americas. My thinking was that the programs would encourage international cooperation and save each station money in their budgets. In the end, nearly twenty stations agreed to participate in the plan. Another group of stations in Brazil created a satellite channel for the Novo Tempo network of stations in that country.

"This is the first international radio network by satellite sponsored by the world church," claimed Jacobsen. The recordings would be sent to the Adventist Global Communication Network in Nova Friburgo, Brazil. From there, they would be sent out by satellite to all the stations in Central and South America. "AWR is committed to broadcasting the gospel by whatever means is the most effective and cost-efficient. We are excited about this new endeavor." He added, "It is truly a message 'fly[ing] in the midst of heaven' " (Revelation 14:6).

Satellite technology was used not only to distribute programming to local stations but also became our most efficient method of distributing programs to AWR shortwave stations. Those broadcasts continued to reach those distant spots where local station licenses couldn't be obtained. And there were many.

In 1999, Don Jacobsen traveled to China with AWR board chair Philip Follett to see for themselves what AWR was doing for the church in that large country. "We met with about a hundred of our listeners in half a dozen cities," Jacobsen reported. "We came away from our visit with renewed gratitude to God for providing His end-time church with the marvelous tool of radio."

One church elder told Don that he had become a Christian by listening to the broadcasts. And then he looked for a year, trying to find a *Voice of Hope* church. He was finally led to an Adventist church and is now an elder in that church. He said, "I looked for a year to find a Sabbath keeping church, but AWR held me till I found it."

Miss Lee, a young woman in her early thirties, is a pastor in training. She told Jacobsen how she duplicates AWR broadcast schedules by the hundreds and distributes them everywhere she goes. She said, "I feel this is an important part of my ministry. In many places, we have no pastor and must rely entirely on radio—for evangelism and for training lay workers."

In another city, Jacobsen and Follett spoke with two local elders who both became Christians through listening to AWR. One of them said, "AWR presents a practical Christianity. We learned that although we have problems to go through, we also have a Guide, Jesus, who will go with us." The other man said, "We would not have a church here—sixty members—if it weren't for AWR."

"AWR's 123 hours of weekly broadcasts to China serve as the 'glue' that gives cohesion and brings consistency to our people's understanding of Scripture," said Follett. "Day after day, they all hear the same biblical teaching. The broadcasts of AWR serve more than any other single factor to tie our Chinese members into the world church family."

An interesting occurrence took place in Vietnam. Late in the morning on a hot and humid day, a group of people arrived on the beach with their swimsuits and towels. With much laughter and talking, they set up a tent. A second group arrived with food and was welcomed loudly and cheerfully by the first group. They all entered the water, where they swam and dove and floated on the peaceful sea.

If bystanders had been watching very carefully, they would have seen the swimmers, one by one, approach a certain man, remain with him for a brief time, and then swim away. But what the onlookers probably would not have guessed is that those swimmers were being baptized by the speaker of our AWR broadcast to that country.

Joy pervaded the happy group when they returned to shore and during the welcome ceremony that followed. Some of those people had waited three years to be baptized. "Now they are God's children and are receiving the power of the Holy Spirit to witness for Jesus," their radio pastor said. Because of conditions in the country at the time, he thought it wise not to tell us how many people he baptized that day, but it was enough to start a whole new church of happy believers.

Twenty-Four

A South Pacific Assignment

At the dawn of the twenty-first century, AWR was broadcasting twelve hundred hours a week—171 hours a day in nearly fifty languages. Maintaining contact with the current operations and adding more as growth spread around the world were huge tasks for our small team of administrators. I found myself on airplanes frequently, and I discovered, once I got time to stop and think, that my work took me away from home 50 percent of the time. For me, it was a heavy load. I began dreaming of a job that wouldn't require constant travel.

One day, while looking at job opportunities online, I came across an announcement that Avondale College (now Avondale University) in Australia was looking for someone to start a communication program there. I halfheartedly sent a query, not expecting much to come of it. However, in a short time, I received an invitation to come and join the faculty as head of their new program for a bachelor of arts in Communication. Attracted to the possibility of working at a place where I wouldn't be required to constantly roam the earth, I responded with definite interest. Andrea and I talked it over and decided it would be a good move.

The next few weeks were full of trips from our home in Binfield to the Australian High Commission in downtown London. The school

A South Pacific Assignment

year would start at Avondale in Australia's fall—spring in the Northern Hemisphere—and the deadline to obtain a work permit so I could arrive in time for the start of classes was fast approaching. Finally, the document arrived, allowing us to make travel plans; I would only be a month late for the start of classes. With the permit, I was surprised to find a letter inviting me to become an Australian citizen in two years!

As we prepared to pack our belongings once again to move to the other side of the world, we began to reminisce about our twenty-year connection with the wonderful ministry of AWR: staff members who became friends, the hundreds of listeners we had the privilege of connecting with in a personal way, and members of the churches where we were members. The nostalgia was overwhelming, but the thrill of starting a new adventure balanced the melancholy and the rigors of another move.

Meanwhile, reports from AWR indicated it was still in an expansive growth period. Efforts to expand the church's media outreach now included the many new local stations that were springing up in a number of countries. The use of satellite internet technology to distribute AWR programs was also increasing rapidly. There were some expectations that shortwave would soon disappear, but AWR quickly ascertained that those predictions were unfounded. Large areas of the world were still best reached by that medium. In the words of Don Jacobsen, AWR had to use multimedia because one media could not meet every condition required to reach everyone, and that fact would continue into the future.

Akinori Kaibe, AWR's Asia region director, said, "Most of my area of the world is still only reachable by shortwave." He also said an explosion of internet users in China, for example, caused many broadcasters to exploit that medium, including AWR's program partners for Mandarin Chinese. The few people fortunate enough to have computer access could now listen to Adventist programs through their computers. "But there are still millions of people in China who use only shortwave

Benjamin D. Schoun,
AWR president,
2002–2010.

to get their information," he said. He referenced a recent audience survey in part of China that revealed AWR had more than 1.1 million listeners on shortwave.

The changes in preferred media were more apparent in Europe, where satellite became the dominant medium for program distribution to local stations that were coming on the air. Bert Smit, AWR's Europe region director, said, "We've been on digital stereo satellite in Europe for almost two years in English and German. In 2000 we will expand our satellite distribution system to a full twenty-four-hour feed in many languages to serve local FM stations in Europe."

Even with the advent of local station affiliates in various European countries, AWR's service of program production training and program distribution was needed. My own prediction was that the broad, worldwide experience of our AWR staff would continue to be needed as Adventist broadcasting expanded.

An illustration of this came in a discussion I had with church leaders in Romania. "We would like to take the government up on the offer of having our own station, but we're not sure what to do," a colleague said. "The government says up to a maximum of six licenses will be permitted for each organization that applies. We think that if we apply for one license, we will get at least one. What do you think?"

I urged him, "Go ahead and apply for six; the Lord will support you."

To their shock, they were awarded the maximum number of licenses. They were eventually able to add four more so that all the major cities of the country had a *Voice of Hope* radio station.

"Africa is still a shortwave continent," said Samuel Misiani, AWR's Africa region director. However, he reported, "Very cautiously, some governments are permitting local religious stations to come on the air—and the Adventist Church is working to take advantage of those opportunities—but for now, shortwave is the prime way to reach all the continent."

AWR was leasing airtime on a large Sentech shortwave station in South Africa to reach East, Central, and West Africa. Another station was being leased in Madagascar, and stations leased in Europe were still covering North Africa.

"Satellite program distribution to over forty stations in the Americas is the best way to reach listeners these days," reported Greg Scott, region director for the Americas. "We're having great success with our

A South Pacific Assignment

satellite network in Spanish. The stations currently downlinking AWR programs by satellite will grow to more than fifty within two years. We have local stations in most Spanish-speaking countries. Cuba and Mexico are two exceptions, so we will continue to broadcast to Mexico and the Caribbean by shortwave," he added. A Portuguese network for twenty church-owned stations in Brazil was accessing programs from the same satellite.

Don Jacobsen predicted AWR would be adding one new language to the program schedule every month in 2000. He said, "Just twenty languages are spoken as a first language by over three billion people—that's half the world's population. And AWR is broadcasting in seventeen of those twenty top languages." There was more behind AWR's success than just transmission power. Producers around the world were generating programs of value that spoke to the heart of listeners. Many remarkable stories came as a result of their efforts.

Salai is a teacher in a remote village in Myanmar "that is five days from the nearest road." He wrote, "The bus along that route may come once a week or twice a month." He went on to describe his location:

> If there is no bus, it's a 96-mile walk to the nearest town and shops. There are 25 homes in the village. All are animists, except me, I'm an elementary school teacher, and I am a Christian.
>
> I accepted Jesus as my personal Savior when I was a teenager, but I had very little knowledge of the Bible. Now, because of the program *Search for Happiness* on AWR, I am totally changed from my past life, and I have been sharing the *Search for Happiness* message with my students. Now the children take their Bible lessons home, and it seems the parents and even the village head wants to know more about Jesus.

A similar program, named *Passion for Life*, was being aired in China. This one-hour program, broadcast on the air daily from the Guam shortwave station, targeted young adults, twenty to thirty-five years old. The program producer was Zhao Ming, who recorded his show at the studios in Hong Kong. He divided his program into two parts: The first half hour was a class in English as a second language, using topics of interest to young people. "In the second part of the program," Zhao said, "I talk about many things: study, work, dating, marriage, psychology, relationship skills, comparative religion, Bible study, faith, how to deal with difficulties, health—whatever we think will interest young people. Most of the topics are from questions that young people write about in their letters to us."

One message from a young lady named Yong Mei, who lives in Shanghai, was indicative of the responses to the program. "Last night, I was weeping as I turned on the radio. The first thing I heard was your voice telling me how to seek peace in times of difficulty. I listened carefully—it seemed that God arranged this program just for me! Your words encouraged me a lot because I have been going through a lot of difficulties lately."

She went on to say, "After the program, I dried my tears, and my heart was lifted. I said to myself: 'God is love, and I want to put my burden in His hand. He will give me faith and strength to face all these difficulties in life.' "

Zhao was able to contact a church member in Shanghai who visited Yong Mei and introduced her to a church family in the city.

John, writing from India, told AWR about hearing a program that shared the story of Job from the Bible—a man who lost everything, even his family. John could identify with Job's life.

Dowell Chow, AWR president, 2010–2016.

His tale of woe seemed never ending. He retired from the army and invested all his savings in a business. But he failed miserably and had no more money. In the meantime, he lost a leg in an accident. He couldn't find a job and became a burden to his family. Then his wife left him, and his children were scattered.

He said, "I lived in a hopeless, helpless situation; I had no desire to live." While he was in this "deep valley of agony," he said, "by accident," he tuned into the AWR Tamil program. That day the message was on the life and suffering of Job. "It was the turning point in my life; I began to focus on the positive side of my life. I learned that day that the Lord, who stood beside Job in his dark hours, is surely present in my life too."

"This may be only the third or fourth letter I have written in my entire life," began a letter from Abdulla, who lived in a North African country. "I have found comfort in your programs, whose friendly radio waves I started hearing two weeks ago."

Then Abdulla described his situation. He was from a poor family, had four brothers and a sister, and, at twenty-one years old, was the eldest. They lived in a remote place where transportation was difficult, except on market day. Abdulla was a first- and second-grade teacher. He previously had no interest in listening to the radio, but now he wrote, "Radio has become my only friend." The radio he used to listen to the *Voice of Hope* was not his own. A student loaned it to him because Abdulla's hashish addiction drained his salary every month, and he never had enough money to buy a radio.

"At 18, I became addicted to hashish, which has made me unsociable and lonely. I find all my comfort in the drug, while inside, I am crying blood tears." He asked for religious literature and the health booklets offered on the AWR program. He added, "Please send me the Holy Bible, too, because I am in extreme need of it." He then relayed how he found enough money to send his rare letter: "I had to sacrifice a gram of hashish to buy the stamp."

One of the best tributes to the quality of AWR programs came from a listener in Japan. Mr. Tsutomu Hakozaki openly declared he did not appreciate any religious programs. It seemed the more he heard, the more he hated them! However, upon hearing AWR, his attitude changed. He said he had "such a pure feeling" listening to the announcer's voice, and the program was "so different from other religious broadcasts" that he became a faithful follower and believer.

Twenty-Five

Time in Oz

It was spring when I arrived in Cooranbong, New South Wales, in the land that locals call Oz. It's a place where everyone is considered equal, and people are always ready to remind you of that equality. Everyone calls you "mate," but this practice made me lazy because I didn't have to remember names anymore. Everyone was a mate! It wasn't a new term for me because I heard people call others "mate" in England, but it was usually reserved for someone special—a close or intimate friend—whereas in Oz, everyone and anyone is a mate.

From the Sydney Airport, I rushed down to Avondale College because classes were already underway. I was eager to relieve John Cox, the academic dean, who was conducting my classes until I could arrive. Andrea stayed behind in Binfield to care for the final details of our house sale and then made a stop in the United States to visit family on her way Down Under. I was provided temporary quarters in a vacant unit of a duplex on the two-lane road leading into campus. Upon waking my first morning there, I sensed I was being watched through the window.

Looking out from behind my curtain, I could see two big brown eyes. It was a cow, just checking me out. The house was at the edge of a meadow where a herd of cattle grazed. I learned later that a local farmer was leasing the pasture from the university for his herd of dairy cows.

When Andrea did arrive some weeks later, we were offered a permanent home about a block away, closer to Dora Creek, which is a small river that circles half the campus. Locals said they often saw platypuses splashing in the creek.

Avondale College was full of friendly people, and my experience from day one was pleasant. The camaraderie of the faculty was one thing that I came to cherish. We met together frequently and equally shared the respect we had for each other's conscientious contributions to the academic experience. We met at the end of each quarter to defend, or justify, the grades we were giving our students. We also had our grades reviewed by an external examiner for evaluation.

I was assigned an office in Bethel Hall, a historic building in the middle of campus. It was a two-story wooden structure—one of the first two buildings constructed when Avondale College was founded in 1897. Ellen G. White, an early leader in the Seventh-day Adventist Church, was a major promoter of the college. She had a home just off campus called Sunnyside. A story is told that she often came over to the campus to help with the construction of the building, usually wielding a hammer to help drive nails. She was also known to have visited farmers in the vicinity whenever she heard one of their family members was ill.

When Andrea arrived, she was assigned an office next to mine. She would be continuing her public relations work for AWR remotely for nearly a year. Although my class schedule was busy, I enjoyed staying on campus without the stress of catching the next airplane. Our team was also installing a suite of computers for students to use in radio and video production. Next door, we had an audio-video production studio.

My students came from most of the Australian states and territories as well as from countries overseas. One of my favorite activities with them was spending an evening every week in Cabramatta, a suburb of Sydney, feeding homeless people and interacting with drug users. Four students would jump into my car after classes on Friday, and we would travel down the motorway just over an hour's drive in the big city of Sydney, then circle downtown to the western suburb where the church had a mission in a storefront building. It was rewarding to prepare food for those who came in and to do our best to befriend them in the hope that they would give up their drug habits. If they agreed to try to quit, we would make reservations for them in a rehabilitation facility where they could detox and, hopefully, give up the addiction.

Another frequent activity was church visitation. One of the professors was charged with organizing speakers for churches around the state of New South Wales on weekends. Andrea and I enjoyed our road trips off campus to visit area churches. It was a great way to get acquainted with the country and an enjoyable break from the academic environment. Our visits through the outback to country towns were both educational and relaxing.

I had been teaching for five years when I was given the job of development director in addition to my teaching. John Cox, now president of Avondale College, joined me in visiting friends of the school—usually graduates—to seek funding for projects on campus. We included one trip to the United States to visit potential donors there. We were able to obtain funds for improvements to buildings, including a new roof for a dormitory, several new classroom interiors, and other minor projects.

In my sixth year at Avondale College, Pastor Laurie Evans stopped by my office to learn more about our communication training program. He was president of the church's South Pacific Division—one of thirteen administrative subdivisions of the world church. (The South Pacific Division's territory included Australia, New Zealand, and all the island nations south of the equator in the Pacific Ocean.) He stopped by occasionally to chat casually about media training and my views on how the church could use various media to advance its mission.

I enjoyed the chats, but it soon became evident he had a specific reason for grilling me about the challenges of using media. He eventually asked if I would be willing to join his staff and lead the division's communication efforts. His goal was unique because he wanted to do something no other arm of the church had done before: combine all the church's media endeavors into one overarching organization. His idea was to join the division's Communication Department, the Adventist Media Center in Australia, and Signs Publishing into one entity: the Adventist Media Network. I was asked to be the network's chief executive officer.

The new job meant another move for Andrea and me; this time to the big city—actually to Wahroonga, a suburb of Sydney. Headquarters for the network would be in the modern, glass-fronted media center next to the church's main office on Fox Valley Road. In our building were the large video and audio studios, the Bible correspondence school, and the offices for church publications, a marketing director, and administrative staff. Our second campus was the Signs Publishing Company in Warburton, near Melbourne, in the state of Victoria in southern Australia.

Also located in Wahroonga was Sydney Adventist Hospital, which is a major medical center in the city. Andrea began working part time for the School of Nursing that Avondale College operated next to the hospital. Her primary responsibilities revolved around scheduling students for practical experience in area hospitals.

Our new family digs were across a small streamed connected to the hospital grounds by a walkway, which descended precipitously down into a semitropical garden where we passed tiny wild orchids and other flowering plants. From there, we crossed a footbridge and then labored up the opposite bank to the hospital. It provided good exercise and a quick way to work that would otherwise require a lengthy car ride through city traffic. As in Cooranbong, the large colorful parrots and other birds found across the country were ever present. Whereas kookaburras seemed more plentiful on the main college campus, here in the city, cockatoos ruled. The air was constantly filled with their squawks.

Among our triumphs in the media work were the successful consolidation of all the South Pacific Division's communication entities into one network, the introduction of a system using satellite to provide web pages for all churches in the South Pacific, and the start-up of a number of radio stations in the island nations. As in other parts of the world, satellite technology largely determined the church's advance in the world of media.

At AWR, two presidents followed Don Jacobsen while we were busy Down Under. In 2002, Benjamin Schoun was appointed and served the longest of any of AWR's presidents until 2010, when Dowell Chow took over. In 2017, Duane McKey became president, and during his term, I would again become directly involved with AWR.

Twenty-Six

Back in the USA

"It's time we think about moving back to the USA," I said to Andrea one midsummer day when I was in a contemplative mood. My retirement was on the horizon—just over a year away—and since we were vested in the American Social Security system, it was time to plan our next stage in life that would need to be back in America. Retirement didn't seem enticing to me. I felt strong enough to carry on getting the good news out to the South Pacific nations, and we both loved Australia. Would retirement put me on the back shelf? For the first time in my career, I felt a little anxiety about the future.

I followed my comment with a question, spoken as much to myself as to her: "How does one seek a position on the other side of the planet at my age?" She answered matter-of-factly: "You'll just have to start from scratch—there's the internet." The next day I sat down at the computer and began my search.

I checked job listings for all the church entities I could think of, but nothing seemed to pop out at me. After several hours of searching, I gave up for the day and whispered, "God, please show me the way." He had never failed me in the past. For twenty years with AWR, I simply went wherever I was told. I was also sure He led me to Australia, where I faced one of the biggest challenges of my life—launching the

Back in the USA

Adventist Media Network. Once again, I was waiting for His call.

A few days later, I was at the computer again when I realized there was one other list of employment opportunities in the church system that I hadn't tried: academic institutions. I went through the list, one by one, when suddenly one screamed at me in bold letters: Andrews University was seeking a lecturer in its communication department for one year! I whooped and hollered for my wife. "I found it; I found it," I yelled.

She came running in. "What did you find?"

"Andrews University wants a communication lecturer for one year," I said excitedly. "That's it."

She was speechless. Could it be we might go back to our early academic roots, where we still had friends and where we spent nine of our intellectual growth years?

I stayed at the computer and immediately composed a job application and attached my résumé.

There was no response. I agonized and fretted for days. "God, it seems You provided this job opening just for me. Will You make it come true?" I just had to leave it in His hands. Then the response came: "Yes, we want you."

Over and over, I said, "Thank You, Father. You came to my rescue again." It was another "send me" moment. We announced our decision to the division's leaders and started planning our move halfway around the world. Our longest time in one place—eight years in Australia—was about to come to an end.

My farewell party in the media center's social room was emotional. What dear friends and colleagues I was leaving. Andrea's team at the nursing school also planned a farewell lunch for her. As a going-away gift, I was presented with a large framed photograph of a small tin-roofed stone shack in the middle of the outback desert. It was titled *No Longer at This Address* by the photographer. *How appropriate*, I thought. *How many times over the years have we left old addresses behind?* That photograph has hung in a prominent place in our home ever since.

Our flights to Los Angeles were booked separately. Our dog, Toby, and I would be on an airline that permitted the transport of pets, while Andrea would be on a different flight on the same day at about the same time. At the airport, we suddenly heard an announcement: my flight with Toby would be delayed twenty hours until the next day. We were able to get my flight transferred, but Toby had to stay overnight before he could board again the next day. Fourteen hours later, Andrea and I landed safely in Los Angeles and found a room with friends for the night.

The next day we went to the cargo warehouse to pick up our little dog. After a couple of hours of dealing with paperwork, we were told we could go to the cargo bay to pick up our precious little friend. The huge garage door slowly creaked open, and sitting alone in the middle of the entrance was the little carrier with Toby. He seemed a bit dazed when we first lifted him from the carrier, but soon he was showering us with kisses.

Thanks to a local family who happened to have an empty house for rent next to the Andrews University campus, we had a place to temporarily call home as soon as we arrived in Berrien Springs, Michigan. It was close enough, on the banks of Lemon Creek, so that I could walk up the hill and cross the campus playing fields to my office in the Department of Communication. During our careers, this familiar ground was the only place we returned to live a second time.

I was soon busy serving as an academic counselor and teaching classes on public speaking, public relations, journalism, and Interpersonal Communication to undergraduates and teaching Communication Theories to graduate students. Andrea enjoyed canning applesauce, renewing friendships with former friends, and taking in the public lectures and concerts offered at the university.

While living in Michigan, several opportunities opened for us to visit Andrea's sister in Albuquerque, New Mexico. Those visits solidified our plan to move to the Southwest for retirement. We liked the high desert, constant sunshine, and blue skies in the "Land of Enchantment." We especially fell in love with the capital city, Santa Fe. We felt at home there whenever we visited, probably because it was so different from the rest of the country. With the American Indian and Spanish influences, it seemed to us like a completely different country. We had experienced and enjoyed a number of different cultures, and we decided we would like to add one more cultural experience to our lives.

All too soon, our year at Andrews ended. However, I agreed to stay another six months to help the Department of Communication until a new professor could be installed. Meanwhile, our dream of settling in the West was intensifying. By Christmas of 2009, we couldn't wait

Back in the USA

A highlight of AWR's fiftieth anniversary in 2021 was the reconciliation between the Philippine government and the New People's Army on the island of Mindoro. After more than fifty years of battle, the war stopped, and thousands of rebels and many military became Seventh-day Adventists. The photo shows one of the baptisms in Palawan.

to pack our bags and head to our retirement destination. We drove off the Andrews campus just as a winter snowstorm was about to hit.

We were delighted with Santa Fe, our ninth "hometown" since we got married. The clear air and our house, with its views of the Sangre de Cristo Range of the Rocky Mountains to the east and the Jemez Mountains to the west, made us feel like we were on an extended vacation in a mountain hideaway. Behind our house was the Arroyo de los Chamisos, a usually dry creek bed where coyotes roamed. Their howls at the moon in the night and their scat on the walking trail along the dry creek bed were a touch of the wild that we had never experienced before. Newspaper stories of bears visiting the city and reports of an occasional mountain lion tracking the arroyo beds around town added to the exotic experience of living in the high desert.

We remembered that there were four Adventist churches in the area, two Spanish and two English. Our chosen church congregation was friendly and gracious, so we soon had a new church family. As always, I was concerned for the lovely children in the church. With the help of Adrian Martinez, a military veteran and good friend, we started a Pathfinder Club. Then, with a group of other concerned members, we were able to start a church school for kindergarten through eighth grade. As with most retirees, we were free to go through the discovery process of deciding what would come next. For many people, it is that scary time when they have to invent a new career so they can stay active.

I was enthralled with the history of the city and discovered it is one of the most visited small cities in America. The downtown plaza is always buzzing with tourists. The architecture and ambiance make it one of the most distinctive cities in the United States. It is the oldest capital city in the country, as well as the highest capital city at over seven thousand feet. We soon were mesmerized by the atmosphere of its laid-back style, ancient history, huge art colony, and major cultures it embraces—American Indian, Spanish, Mexican, and American.

"Look, here's a newspaper announcement you may be interested in," Andrea said one day. She obviously had noticed my need to get involved in something challenging after nearly two years of total freedom. The announcement was about a hospitality convention to be held at the downtown convention center. "You've enjoyed learning about the history here; why don't you go and see if you find anything of interest?"

In the large exhibition hall of the building were several dozen booths featuring hotels, restaurants, events, and state and local parks. I wandered the booths and eventually came upon one that said "Tour Guides." I blurted out to the man in the booth, "I would like to be a tour guide!" He smiled, told me about the life of a tour guide, and suggested I join him on one of his history tours.

My first walking tour of downtown Santa Fe was fascinating. We visited the old historic hotel, the La Fonda; the central plaza; the courtyards of Palace Avenue; the Cathedral Basilica of St. Francis; the Loretto Chapel; and the oldest house and oldest church. "This is for me," I said to Peter, the tour guide, at the end.

"Well, then what we want to do next is have you conduct a tour with another tour guide to see how well you do."

I rushed home to frantically study up on Santa Fe history.

My tour was set for three days later. A seasoned tour guide—a lovely woman with a cowgirl skirt and western hat—was there to meet me.

Back in the USA

We walked through the downtown just as I had done a few days earlier while I pointed out the historical significance of each corner and courtyard. At the end of the tour, my evaluator said, "You did a good job." I was now qualified to be a Santa Fe tour guide. Eventually, I became the president of the Santa Fe Professional Tour Guide Association. But AWR was about to call again.

In the spring of 2018, the message came: "Would you be willing to serve as our AWR representative in New Mexico?" Sue Hinkle, whom I met when she was communication director in the Texico Conference where we now lived, was working at AWR on an assignment to organize field representatives—"Ambassadors"—for the church's international radio ministry. There was no way I could refuse, having nurtured the ministry of AWR for most of my life.

I soon learned that under the leadership of Duane McKey, AWR was now a multipronged ministry. Its new watchword was "Broadcast to Baptism." This new motto clearly indicated not only spreading the Word but also leading new believers to a local church family. Public evangelism meetings would be conducted using AWR leadership, and the broadcasters themselves would participate in public meetings in addition to introducing listeners to the Adventist message via the ether waves.

The organization's outreach was widely expanded to accomplish this greater mission. In addition to shortwave, AWR's vision now encompassed local radio stations on AM, FM, and medium wave. Thanks to satellite technology, the ministry also expanded to extensive use of the internet with evangelistic programs on social media platforms, such as Facebook and YouTube. A new idea for utilizing cell phone technology to share spiritual messages with one's friends was heralded as "cell phone evangelism." It was first brought to the attention of AWR by Neville Neveling, a church member in Namibia.

Another new technology engaged by AWR was solar technology. A device they called a "Godpod" was adopted as a way to distribute the gospel message. *Godpods* are small handheld devices that look like transistor radios on which hours and hours of programs, even readings of the entire Bible, are recorded. An individual can recharge the device simply by letting it sit in the sunlight for several hours. These are given out to various people groups that may be in remote areas where radio signals do not reach or to individuals who cannot purchase or operate a radio due to physical inability.

"This ministry has undergone a big shift over the years," explained McKey. "As technology has changed, AWR has adjusted with distribution methods that better address the different regions we cover. We believe we need to share with all the world via all media platforms."

To facilitate this new wide-ranging mission, AWR began sponsoring mass meetings around the world, encouraging Adventist broadcasters and church members to get involved in the process. A new administrative initiative called Total Member Involvement was adopted by AWR. Its goal is to recruit thousands of church members to participate and even preach at mass meetings around the world.

At the church's world headquarters, President Ted Wilson called AWR's new emphasis "one of the most aggressive evangelistic outreach endeavors at the end of time."

In 2021, AWR celebrated fifty years of broadcasting, and in that year, one of the most incredible events ever witnessed by the church occurred. It happened in the Philippines, on the island of Mindoro. An armed group of Communist soldiers called the New People's Army, better known as the NPA, were camped on the island in the mountain jungles. For more than fifty years, they had been fighting the government in a conflict that claimed the lives of more than forty thousand people.

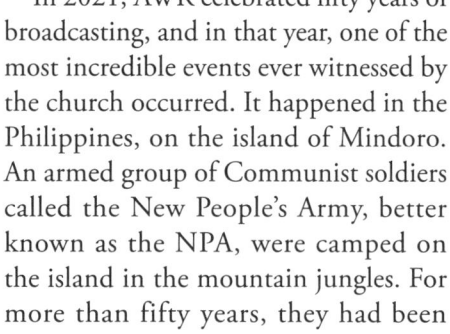

Duane McKey became the sixth AWR president in 2017.

An Adventist pastor on the island, Robert Dulai, was surprised to find visitors at his house one day. Members of the NPA had come to tell him their lives had been changed by the messages they heard over AWR. AWR had been beaming the gospel message by radio into Mindoro and across the entire country. Not only did these messages of hope change the hearts of those hardened soldiers and assassins, but it was the beginning of a transformation for the whole country.

The subsequent chain of events would astound AWR's leaders and capture the attention of the Philippines' top government officials. Unexpectedly, more and more rebels were laying down their arms and asking for membership in the Seventh-day Adventist Church. An AWR team paid a visit to the rebel stronghold in the remote mountains. While there, they conducted a medical clinic and a spiritual convocation for the rebels and their families.

Then, in November of 2021, AWR and the church's world headquarters were given special permission by Philippine President Rodrigo Duterte to conduct large evangelistic meetings in Mindoro. Ted Wilson and Duane McKey led a team to the area and witnessed as rebels came by the hundreds to declare their new allegiance to the God of the universe. Members of the government military were moved greatly by the outpouring of reform and remorse that these mountain families demonstrated. Many of them were so moved that they, too, wanted to participate in a mass reconciliation between the two sides.

"For years, we tried everything to end the conflict," said the island's chief of police. "We offered to bribe the rebels with food and a stipend, but nothing we did ever worked. In the end, it was through the work of Adventist World Radio that this was accomplished."

The Adventists knew it was God's doing. What overwhelming joy the AWR staff felt as they saw rebels ask forgiveness and receive asylum from the central government. The military shared their immense relief at the end of the war and joined the rebels in celebrating the transformation that was taking place. President Duterte expressed his gratitude to AWR and the Seventh-day Adventist Church for helping to end the war on Mindoro.

It was an astonishing development, and yet there was a sense that it was far from over. There were indications that other rebel groups on other islands witnessed what happened in Mindoro and began taking steps toward making peace in their districts. The world was witnessing the powerful force of the Almighty, who brings radical change to people's hearts.

Twenty-Seven

The Navajo Call

In my new role as an ambassador for AWR, my assignment was to seek speaking appointments in Seventh-day Adventist churches in New Mexico in order to share the news AWR was constantly generating as it carried out its worldwide agenda. I began a new type of travel—by car—to the distant churches located in different parts of the state, which is the country's fifth largest in land area. Trips could take up to six hours from one corner to the opposite corner of New Mexico.

One day I decided to connect with the Gallup church on the western side of the state. Gallup, a historic old railroad town next to the Navajo Nation, would be my first trip to the far side of the state near the Arizona line. I had an old conference directory and was using it to contact the pastors or head elders of churches to make my appointments. I discovered the Gallup church was without a pastor at the time, and there was no answer at the head elder's telephone number. So I tried the person listed as church treasurer, who did answer. However, he had moved across the state line into Arizona and was a leader at the church in Window Rock, the capital city of the Navajo Nation.

I soon was on the schedule to speak at Window Rock. This was outside of policy: I was supposed to limit my travels only to churches in my assigned state of New Mexico, but since a small part of the city

The Navajo Call

of Window Rock stretched over the line into New Mexico, I decided I should take the speaking appointment.

The main highway from New Mexico into Window Rock turns into a main street of the town. Andrea and I spent the night in what seemed to be the only motel in the downtown area. The next morning our GPS took us from the business district out to the suburb of St. Michaels, Arizona. The church group had recently obtained a vacant lot in exchange with another church, so they were meeting in a modular manufactured building at the front of the lot facing the main highway. It was right next to a restaurant and motel.

We were warmly welcomed and had a very attentive audience. Afterward, as happens at most Adventist gatherings, a fellowship meal was provided. At the meal, a couple of the elders came to me and asked whether we could have a follow-up meeting after lunch. I readily agreed. We returned to the meeting room, and about a dozen people gathered to join the discussion. To my surprise, they said, "We want to have a radio station to reach all the Navajo Nation."

Forever a believer in the power of radio to share God's message, I could only say, "Well, let's see what the Lord will do for you." I had witnessed too many miracles in my work in God's "Air Force" to doubt for a second what God can do. When there is a will, He will provide a way. Thus began a new and wonderful relationship with my Navajo brothers, as well as a gigantic project to keep me busy.

But what am I doing? I thought. The Navajo Nation—the largest American Indian reservation in North America at twenty-seven thousand square miles of high desert—is also the largest tribe in North America at more than 399,000 enrolled members, with upwards of 161,000 people still living on the sprawling reservation or in the surrounding cities. A third of the people live off the grid, with no running water or electricity.

Yes, God, I like to be challenged, but this? The project scope was overwhelming, but God seemed to want this to happen. "So, is that why You sent me here?" I asked the Lord.

Thus began a series of meetings with a planning committee at Window Rock. It became clear as we worked together that a bilingual station, airing both Navajo and English, had the potential to become a tremendous blessing to the Navajo people. Furthermore, the Navajo belief in a Creator and other similarities with Adventist beliefs would be a beautiful fit. The Adventist health message could be of great help in bettering life on the reservation, and our message of hope could create a new vision for this great people. At one meeting, it was decided to call the planned radio station Diné Adventist Radio, "The People's Adventist Radio."

We requested help from AWR for technical expertise, and they sent out Sammy Gregory, a project engineer, to evaluate the site. In researching the requirements for obtaining a radio license, we discovered that the easiest and fastest way to acquire a license would be through the Navajo government. We learned that tribal requests for broadcast licenses were fast-tracked by the FCC in Washington. Our strategy—plan A—would involve negotiating with the tribal government. Yes, the tribe could get a license and lease it to us, but they would be the legal owners.

Our church members on the reservation began seeking the approval of the various regional chapters (equivalent to county governments in most of America) around the reservation. The Adventist Radio project was presented to several chapters where it received endorsements that we planned to pass on to the tribal authorities in the capital.

Then, unexpectedly, in mid-2019, the FCC announced it would conduct an auction for radio licenses, about one hundred of them, around the United States. One license to be auctioned would be in a central location near the middle of the Navajo Nation. Meanwhile, as news of the project spread, private donations from church members around the West, who believed in the importance of the project, began to arrive at the Arizona Conference's office in Scottsdale. The conference soon had enough money to take part in the FCC's auction of radio permits.

So, out of nowhere, we had plan B. But the plans of the FCC fell through in the spring of 2020 when the COVID pandemic hit the world, including the United States. All of a sudden, the FCC announced the auction would be placed on hold indefinitely due to the pandemic.

Our hopes had escalated, and now our disappointment was palpable. We wondered what God was up to. Even though I know His timing is always spot on, this seemed like a missed opportunity. Then, in the summer of 2020, we found out just what God was up to. The FCC spread the word that it would open a window for noncommercial organizations to apply for FM channels in early 2021. That became our next hope—plan C. In the meantime, our people moved forward on a pilot project.

They decided to purchase airtime on KTNN, "The Voice of the Navajo Nation." Church leaders in the Pacific Union Conference provided funds to rent a half-hour slot early on Sunday mornings and to purchase equipment for a studio where the recordings could be made. The Holbrook Seventh-day Adventist Indian School also had a studio provided by AWR some years earlier. We held a three-day virtual training session on Zoom, and fourteen people were trained to make radio programs. At a later training event, seventeen people were trained as radio evangelists.

Two of the local church conferences with Navajo Nation territory in New Mexico helped to fund two small production studios—one in Gallup and the other at La Vida Mission near Farmington—so that American Indian church members would have convenient places to produce programs. The four production centers practiced making the weekly half-hour program, providing the hands-on training required for filling the airwaves 24-7 when we received our own station license.

On August 2, 2020, the first program aired on KTNN. After only six and a half hours on the air, fifty listeners responded, requesting Bible studies and other literature. The response was beyond gratifying, and the listenership grew rapidly. Requests for Bible studies began to arrive from all corners of the reservation and from cities where large concentrations of tribal members had settled outside the reservation, such as Phoenix and Albuquerque. God now had a voice for these special people.

"God is still in the miracle business," I said to Pastor Dale Wolcott, the coordinator of the project on the reservation. He was ably assisted by Pastor Jonathan Chitwood, who coordinated the program production. Under their leadership, the little studio in the Window Rock modular building was performing well. But the dream of having their own station was still in the future.

God was making it clear that we still have a mission to make His voice known in our part of the world. And so it shall always be until the end of this world as we know it. God is still in the business of performing miracles. We prayed, "Lord, just a few more miracles, please."

In late 2021, the FCC finally opened applications for radio station building permits. Four were applied for with the hope that three might be granted: one on the western side of the reservation and one for the center, both in Arizona; and another on the eastern side in New Mexico. Now it was a matter of waiting to see whether our applications would be granted.

The first permit was granted in early January 2022 for a station on the western side of the reservation. The two main cities in the area are Tuba City, the most populous city on the reservation with around nine thousand inhabitants, and Page, on the shore of Lake Powell at the

Arizona-Utah border. Then in April, a second permit was issued by the FCC for a full-power, 100-kilowatt FM station for the village of Piñon at the center of the reservation. Even if a third license was not granted as requested, with two permits, we were confident we would definitely be in the radio-evangelism business. By FCC rules, we're given up to three years to put the stations on the air. A new adventure was about to begin!

* * * * *

Having witnessed God's gift of media as it has been used for sharing His message around the world causes Andrea and me to give all glory to Him. Our love for the mission and ministry of AWR stirs our unceasing gratitude to Him for granting us the privilege of working in God's "Air Force."

How You Can Support Adventist World Radio

Adventist World Radio's mission is to share the Adventist hope in Christ with the hardest-to-reach people in their own language. AWR's family always has room for one more member—and you can be that new member and rejoice in the knowledge that you are helping to make it all possible.

If you have been inspired by the stories of this exciting radio ministry, we invite you to participate in one or more of the following ways:

- Become an AWR Ambassador in your home church
- Become a prayer partner in your circle of friends in support of AWR's mission to reach the world for Jesus
- Sign up to be a digital missionary, and download the AWR360° app at awr.org/apps
- Financially support the work of Adventist World Radio by visiting awr.org/give or by sending your gift to AWR, 12501 Old Columbia Pike, Silver Spring, Maryland 20904, USA

As the incredible stories in this book attest, no one is "impossible to reach" when it comes to the gospel. With no walls, no borders, and no limits, AWR's broadcasts travel where missionaries cannot go—transforming lives for eternity!